SHAMANIC POWER ANIMALS

SHAMANIC
POWER
ANIMALS

EMBRACING THE TEACHINGS
OF OUR NON-HUMAN FRIENDS

DON JOSE RUIZ

Foreword by DON MIGUEL RUIZ, author of *The Four Agreements*

Hierophantpublishing

Cover design by Emma Smith
Cover art by Peratek || Shutterstock
Part Page Illustrations by Varlamova Lydmila and KHIUS || Shutterstock
Medicine Wheel Illustration by Garylarts
Animal Illustrations || Shutterstock
Print book interior design by Frame25 Productions

Hierophant Publishing
8301 Broadway, Suite 219
San Antonio, TX 78209
www.hierophantpublishing.com

If you are unable to order this book from your local bookseller,
you may order directly from the publisher.

Library of Congress Control Number: 2021933209

ISBN 978-1-950253-14-2

10 9 8 7 6 5 4 3 2 1

Being human has always meant
perceiving ourselves in a circle of animals.
—*Paul Shepard*

CONTENTS

FOREWORD

In the Toltec tradition we teach the importance of cultivating respect for the other animals that cohabitate with us on this beautiful planet. We also recognize the power that all animals have to teach us through their characteristics, their behavior, and the wealth of cultural and mythological stories that reveal our interconnection with these amazing creatures since ancient times.

Animal stories also illuminate the fact that out of the astonishingly vast diversity of life on earth, we human animals have been given the added ability to shape our reality through our imagination, language, and manual dexterity. Equipped with these potent gifts, humans can analyze, create, and refine. We build cultures, transform ourselves, and modify nature and the natural world. These are unique powers reserved for the human animal, and we have a responsibility to use these powers wisely and for the benefit of the whole.

Sadly, we know that this is often not the case. Many animals are being harmed and their habitats destroyed as a result of human action and inaction, and any lasting remedy for this will only occur once human beings become willing to look within and make changes based on unconditional love instead of greed and fear.

Of course, as humans, we have also misused our gifts to cause great suffering to ourselves, both externally and internally. We are the only animals that berate ourselves, that compare and reject ourselves, and that judge ourselves as being "not enough." We punish ourselves over and over for the same mistakes, and we take the emotional poison created in the process and inflict pain on others.

Other animals don't do any of this, and in this way they can be our teachers, especially when it comes to the practice of how to live in the present moment. They remind us not to judge, berate, or go against ourselves in any way. Animals are free of these human tendencies, inviting us instead to live in harmony with the way things are.

In this book, my son don José Ruiz shares the wisdom of animals from the depths of his heart. He teaches us that knowledge about the animal world can provide metaphors to help us free our minds and become the artists of our own lives. As you will soon see, unconditional love is the basis for his work.

In these pages, he shows the many ways that we humans can learn from the animal world. At the same time, because we project our own knowledge, emotions, and experiences onto the world around us, working with animals is also a profound way to illuminate the mysteries within ourselves.

For instance, as we observe the behavior of animals, we tend to compare it with our own. We want to be like some animals, to reflect their grace or strength or wisdom. But we may fear other animals or hold their behavior in contempt. In this way, we learn about ourselves and what we want to change about our lives.

That's not to say the wisdom in this book is to be taken as the "final authority." For millennia, we have invented, told, and retold stories about animals and our relationship to them. These can certainly be helpful, but if we aren't careful, we may come to believe that these stories are absolute truth. This is how the mind can turn helpful stories into superstitions, and they can make us susceptible to people who would manipulate us for their own gain.

The Toltec tradition reminds us to free ourselves from all superstitions, including any we may have about the animal world, and to trust in our own intuition instead—something animals have never forgotten.

I hope this book brings love and joy to your life, and that it will hold a special place in your library as an ongoing, insightful resource you'll return to for years to come.

With all my love,

don Miguel Ruiz

INTRODUCTION

When her cub is old enough, Mother Jaguar takes him out into her territory, where she teaches her young one to stalk, swim, hide, and make a home. Seven changes of the season come and go, and soon the cub is ready to venture out on his own.

One day, the young jaguar comes upon a small group of deer. He stalks them cautiously, trying to remember his mother's lessons but feeling unsure of himself. The deer turn and see him, and he falters, staring at them blankly. The deer laugh at him. *Where is your mother? We are not afraid of you!* The jaguar returns home, and for several days he will not go out alone. Instead, he trails behind his mother on her hunts, sullen and feeling small. Finally, she turns on him with a powerful, protective growl. *Do not follow me. I will not hunt with you. You think I am the holder of power, but you are the holder of your own power. Never forget—you are a jaguar.*

As the mother leaps away into the trees, the young jaguar sees clearly. She has shared her knowledge of survival with him, but she has never given him the power he needs to be a jaguar. She can't give him that, even if she wanted to, because that power was always *within him*. From that day onward, he ventures into new territory as a jaguar, filling his belly, keeping balance among the creatures, and fulfilling his destiny.

My father, don Miguel Ruiz, a *Nagual* in our Toltec tradition and the author of *The Four Agreements*, told this story to me and a group of his closest apprentices several years ago. As he concluded the story, he turned to us and said, "You are no longer my apprentices and I am no longer your teacher. Go into the world and chart your own destiny."

I love this story, as well as the context in which my father shared it, for a variety of reasons. First and foremost, it serves as a potent reminder that we all have the power within us, that we are all jaguars. Second, it shows us that learning from others is helpful and even necessary, but there comes a point in our journey when we must go out on our own. Lastly—and this is a point that is often overlooked—this story shows how shamans often use stories involving animals as powerful teaching examples for us. This is by design.

Notice how the jaguar invokes a particular feeling that a mere word cannot. You immediately paint a picture of the scene without even trying. You identify with the jaguar's experience while at the same time observing it from the outside. As we hear the story of the jaguar, we open up emotionally and even physically. It is a simple story on purpose, and it can therefore sink in on a deeper level than any wise saying or list of rules for living. This is the power of animal teachings.

In all of the old stories from every culture on earth, from my ancestors and yours, animals play an important role in the creation of the world itself. They collaborate with their human siblings, speaking in human languages and teaching humans to understand their own animal communications. Birds, bears, rattlesnakes, fish, and insects all share their wisdom in these stories. Animals continue to guide us and share their wisdom even today. Children love the talking animals in cartoons and picture books, and we all grow up soaking in the archetypal wisdom of spiders, pigeons, farm animals, and sea creatures. Yet, as adults, we often forget how to remain open to the same teachings.

For this reason, perhaps we can say that more than in any other wisdom tradition, shamans see the natural world as our great teacher and the animals all around us as the ambassadors of this organic wisdom.

Toltec Shamanism

My family traces its lineage back to the ancient Toltecs, a people who thrived in what is now south-central Mexico between one thousand and three thousand years ago. Like the ancient Vedic cultures of India of the same time period halfway around the world, the Toltecs of Mesoamerica placed their emphasis on what we would today call spirituality, self-realization, or personal transformation.

The Toltec view on these topics was, however, unique in some fascinating ways. For instance, the Toltecs taught that we are all artists. In fact, the very name *Toltec* means "artist" in our native Nahuatl tongue. This is not confined to the traditional understanding of the word as painters, sculptors, or poets. Nor does it only apply to members of my ancestral tribe. This designation extends to every human being on this beautiful planet. The Toltecs believe that every person is an artist, and the art that we create is the story of our life.

Another important word in the Nahuatl language is *nagual*. Like many words in English, *nagual* has two meanings: First, *nagual* is our word for the life force, or the divinity, that is inside you, me, and all things—the thing some might call "spirit," or "source." Second, *Nagual* is used to describe the women and men who served as spiritual teachers in our community. The modern world calls these women and men shamans, so while I am a Nagual in my Toltec tradition, I will refer to myself as a shaman because this term is widely known today.

Since everyone has the nagual energy inside them, we say in the Toltec tradition that everyone has the potential to be a Nagual, or shaman. In one sense, you already are. Simply possessing the gift of being alive in human form means that you have a choice in how you want to live your life. This makes you an artist, a creator. The purpose of Toltec teachings is to wake ourselves up to the power we all hold within.

The shamans in the Toltec tradition, the Naguals, saw animals as powerful teachers in this regard. How? Well, we must start with a foundational truth that Toltecs share with many native and indigenous traditions around the world: the immense respect for our non-human siblings. We see other beings as expressions of the nagual life force in their own right, co-inhabitants of this planet—no better or worse than us, simply different. We are alike in so many ways: we all have a physical body that needs oxygen and water in some form, and of course we all depend on Father Sun and Mother Earth for the nourishment we require to grow and survive.

Yet unlike other animals on the planet, humans have a creative mind that is unmatched, a mind with the power to invent stories about what it perceives. In fact, this storytelling power of the mind happens automatically and without ceasing. This is why, in the Toltec tradition, we say that the mind is constantly dreaming and that our reality is a Personal Dream.

This dreaming mind is the key difference between us and our non-human friends, and it has many positive and negative effects. For instance, on the positive side, you can take a quick look around and marvel at all the things we humans have created. The complex storytelling in our mind leads to insights, inventions, and deeper understanding in all areas of life. We are engineers, builders, explorers, and planners in a way that sets us apart.

However, many of the same technological and material advances made possible by the human mind come at great cost to our ecosystems, our non-human and plant friends, and our own happiness. This is especially true when we fall into habitual use of the most poisonous aspects of the mind, namely greed, jealousy, deceit, disconnection, criticism, and cruelty, among others. While some of these are loosely related to animal experiences—such as the fear of a prey animal or the guile of a camouflaged moth—the human mind has a particular ability to distort these emotions into a kind of poison that we wield against ourselves and others. This poison is the root cause of human suffering.

At its core, Toltec shamanism is based on love, which is the antidote to this poison. Animals teach love in every moment. Sometimes this love is protective like the bear, sometimes unconditional and joyful like that of the little pups

I have at home. Even behind the apparent ruthlessness of the great predators there lies an authentic love for self and a desire to survive and thrive. This love can act as a reminder for us to be clear thinking and focused like the hawk or to protect our most vulnerable parts like the turtle. In this way, animals offer us an invitation to bring love into every part of our dream—especially to any areas where we find we are suffering. After all, love is the power that transforms a bad dream into a beautiful one.

The dreaming mind becomes easily addicted to its own poison, and that's why in my tradition we say that the human mind has an addiction to suffering. As with any addiction, it is reinforced through repetition, and in my view this addiction to suffering is perhaps the greatest problem facing humanity. Because we are so close to it, the concept can be hard to grasp. On some level, most of us understand how substances can establish dominance over our thoughts and behaviors, but are we really getting addicted to misery?

In order to see what I mean, first consider our actions, setting aside our underlying desires or motivations for a moment. We cause suffering in our own lives in all sorts of ways: We work ourselves to the bone to buy things we don't need, and then get angry or sad if we can't have them. We spend time and energy trying to control and influence the behavior of others, and then withhold our love when things don't go our way.

But the deepest misery we inflict on ourselves is self-rejection. We are the only animal on this planet that believes we are not good enough. The rhino does not look at her horn or her folds of protective skin and think, *Ugh*. She is a perfect rhino, just as she is. Humans, on the other hand, will find a way to compare and judge literally any aspect of ourselves—from what's in our bank account to the shape of our nose. Consumed with these judgments, we can get a "hit" of superiority that feels good when we rate ourselves higher than someone else. Inevitably, however, we will be able to find another comparison that knocks us down again and leaves us miserable. Then we try to ease our suffering by getting on top again, shoring up our egos, or denying our deepest truth so that we fit in.

In addition to self-rejection, we humans subject ourselves and each other to a form of powerful control and influence that the Toltecs have named "domestication." Most of us think of this word as it relates to raising and training animals for human benefit, such as domestic farm animals. Toltecs draw yet more wisdom from the animal world by linking animal domestication to the common human practice of training and controlling *ourselves and other people* to act in ways that may not align with our essential natures or our deepest intent. This process begins in childhood, when well-meaning adults tell us to "be quiet" or explain that the singing that brings us pure joy will never be "good enough." We internalize these agreements and pass them on to other humans in turn, adding more suffering to the world.

Addiction to suffering and domestication are games we cannot win, and they tie us to an unending cycle of suffering. Linking our intrinsic worth and happiness to any of our incidental traits is a rejection of our deepest truth, which is that we are all worthy of love. In fact, we are beings of love, and we have the option in every moment to choose love over the poisonous habits of our own mind.

The good news is that because we create most of the suffering we experience in our mind, we also have the means to dismantle this addiction that drains and disconnects us. There is a way to harness the storytelling power of the mind into something beautiful and to let go of the mind's addiction to playing out scenarios that create suffering for ourselves and others. This is a healing path, and the shamans in my family have often used animals as a means to show us the way to this healing.

For example, animals do not fall prey to the same addiction to suffering that the human mind is prone to. They are not bound to the kinds of agreements that distort reality for us. Whenever the shamans in my family noticed themselves or someone else getting caught in the nightmare of the storytelling mind, they would point to the animals for guidance about living free in the present moment. The shamans understood that life only exists in the present moment, where the nagual is. The mind's addiction to suffering very often pulls us out of the present moment to seek peace in the future or to comb through the past to judge and berate ourselves. We think we will be happy only when we acquire this or achieve that or if we had only acted differently in the past. The irony is that this very act of seeking peace outside of the present moment prevents us from finding it. The only place where peace truly exists is the here and now. Animals live this way all the time.

Beyond this essential presence, all animals have the power to inspire, guide, and strengthen our connection to our creative and life-giving powers. In my tradition, as I mentioned, animals are not better than us or worse than us. We are all equal, all part of nature. Any historical, religious, or cultural beliefs that speak of our separateness are not telling the full truth. It's important to embrace this oneness when we seek the wisdom of animals.

How to Use This Book

All animals can hold powerful teachings for us. Ants may demonstrate the power of community; the beetle shares lessons of recycling and regeneration; and the lion imparts its gifts of protective leadership. I could fill many books with the wisdom of animals as I understand it, but the most important thing to remember here is that in the Toltec tradition, we invite you to use your own discernment. Some traditions have very specific rules about how the teachings of animals must be encountered or used. That is not the Toltec way. As in the jaguar story, the power is within you. What is meaningful for you about a certain animal's characteristics or powers may be very different than it is for me. Animal wisdom is just one of many tools in the artistic palette that you can use to create your life. There is no one doctrine here, and the wisdom in these pages draws from nature, science, art, mythology, and various religious and spiritual traditions that are meaningful to me. I encourage you to use what resonates with you.

While we can appreciate the broad variety of wisdom in the animal world, we can also cultivate special relationships with a few particular animals we feel drawn to. These are our power animals, sacred companions that we can call upon to help us on our own unique healing journey. The lessons that they teach and the gifts they share hold special significance for us, and they enjoy a sacred place in our healing work. These animals are our mirrors.

What do I mean by a mirror? The storytelling mind understands things in part through reflection and comparison. Again, this ability can lead to great suffering, but when we understand this aspect of the storytelling mind, we can use it as a tool to our great benefit. When it comes to power animals, this means that we can investigate how each of the traits of a particular animal reflects an inner aspect of ourselves. The qualities we see in animals, the feelings they invoke inside us, both positive and negative, are also within us. If they were not, we could not see them in the animal. Animals can remind us what we want to cultivate and what we want to let go of. Their traits may point to a specific strength in us, or they may highlight a particular blind spot for us.

What's more, we can work with our power animals in ways that go far beyond our glancing or momentary surface understanding of things. In fact, we might not know why a certain animal is so important for us. We don't need to grasp everything with our conscious mind to honor the sacred aspect of animal medicine. Animal medicine often works on a deeper level, revealing itself through knowledge in the body, synchronicity, connection, and profound imaginative capacities.

We might feel a kinship in our body to the melting softness of the happy dog who greets us at the threshold of our home, and we might be inspired by the unconditional love she offers us. We might have a dream of flying that frightens us or, in contrast, makes us feel unfathomably free. We might experience a stinging or tingling sensation with no clear origin—a "bite" from an invisible insect that brings us back into the present moment. During a time of difficult transition, we may begin to feel that we are like the caterpillar, who builds its cocoon and then dissolves into a goo, a complete undoing of identity that allows for the emergence of a new, winged form. These are all deep reflections of animal knowledge that can guide the opening of our energetic bodies and minds and that can enhance our understanding of the different passages and paths of our lives. The path of the power animal is therefore a path to our own personal power—one that respects all animals as sacred guides.

Finally, because animals are our mirror, they can also be our healers. When we heal ourselves and our Personal Dream using the wisdom of animals, we contribute to healing the broken systems that might seem far beyond our direct personal influence. In fact, the animal world needs us to help heal the planet from the negativity, pain, and destruction that the human mind has inflicted on the Dream of the Planet.

The beginning of this book provides some basic teachings about how you can work with power animals. Animals can provide inspiration, offer potent symbols for various times in our lives, and bolster our strengths and help us understand our weaknesses. Power animals can guide decision-making by helping us uncover the meaning of certain experiences. In the Toltec tradition, we recognize that different animals may reflect different stages of life. Some animal teachers may come and go, and others may stay with you and act as guides throughout your life. Don't worry about working with the "right" animals or about working with animal medicine in the "right" way.

I hope that this book will be a companion on your journey, one whose wisdom you can turn to again and again. For that reason, Part Two contains information relating to specific animals. Some entries include some of the mythological, religious, or cultural stories built over generations of animal observation, which can tell us something about the gifts these animals have offered our ancestors and that still have meaning for us today. As I will explain in Part One, each animal aligns with a specific quadrant in the medicine wheel and a specific element of the natural world. Many of the entries include scientific facts and contemporary cultural references, because Toltec shamanism embraces an evolving understanding of the age in which we live and values all available tools in the healing and creative process. In so many ways, the living world holds an important place in our lives as shamans, and power animals can help us in our greater journey toward healing and alignment with the nagual.

It is my hope that these pages will be a gateway into the awesome power of animals. May you soar and roar, dig down into the earth and dive deep into ocean currents. May you build and weave, protect and restore, at all times perceiving the living world in new ways and opening to new insights. May you carry the teachings of our scaled, furred, and feathered siblings on your journey of healing and wholeness, and may these lessons guide you as you break free from the human mind's addiction to suffering and claim your birthright as the artist of your own life.

Similarly, every being on earth—everything from amoebas to mountains—is also a creator of reality. No person or animal or facet of nature is better or worse, more or less of an artist than another. Each of us has a Personal Dream, a story we are telling ourselves, and together we have a collective story, the Dream of the Planet. That means all of us are cocreating the reality of life on earth and even in the universe as a whole. Consciousness itself is the storytelling energy that makes the universe hum.

PART ONE

KEY TOOLS FOR WORKING WITH POWER ANIMALS

Creatures are all around us; animals of wing and scale, skin and feather. I'm talking about all the animals you can think of: Wild ones who thrill our hearts and stand our hair on end. Animals of the waters, from tiny fish in shallow streams to strange beings who live only in the unfathomable depths of the ocean. Winged creatures and birds whose very form and shape remind us of what is eternal and feels connected to the creation of the world. In so many ways, animals remain unknown to us. We can't see through their eyes or know what it's like to exist in bodies that are so different from our own. And yet they remain our companions in all ways. We share our home and we all have the same mother, the earth. Even our body itself could be thought to be an organism made up in part of millions of separate microscopic animals living together. We are a kind of continent unto ourselves—a walking biome.

In addition to their powerful physical presence in our lives, animals hold sacred space in our psyche. If we choose to ignore the gifts of animals or minimize interaction with their wisdom, we miss out on an essential part of being human. Once we open up to the idea of animal teachings, however, the possibilities are limitless. Let's look at a few of the many ways that you can work with animal wisdom and connect to the natural world, to set you on the path to increasing your power and connection to the nagual within.

Animal wisdom provides guidance for every stage of life and can be called upon to help us as we embark on a new journey, tackle particular challenges, or make decisions large or small. Animals can help us celebrate and express our gratitude for the natural world. Through animal medicine, we unlock the powers of synchronicity and imagination that can aid us in bringing clarity and joy to our lives and freeing our storytelling minds from suffering. This is one of the ways that animals are healers—they can activate a deep intrinsic wisdom within us that is so often quieted by the forces of domestication and the mind's addiction to suffering. We will also look at the ways in which using ritual and physical objects such as medicine bags and personal altars can make animal wisdom more concrete and usable.

These areas of exploration can be applied to any of the specific animals that make up the rest of this book, and indeed to any other animal you connect with out in the world or within your inner imaginative landscape. At the end of this section, there are three exercises to get you started with power animals and moving into the mindset of learning and growing from these sacred siblings.

The Medicine Wheel

One of the most well-known symbols in shamanism is the medicine wheel, a circle with no beginning and no end. For the native peoples of North and South America, this ancient symbol has been an integral part of spiritual life. It contains the cardinal directions of north, east, south, and west, and each direction is traditionally associated with an element, a color, and a season, as well as life cycle stages and aspects of the self. The medicine wheel is a physical object represented in symbolic artwork, and the image of the wheel is built into landmarks at sacred locations, which are often meeting places for communal ceremonies and rites. The medicine wheel is also an internal idea, a powerful metaphor that guides and brings balance.

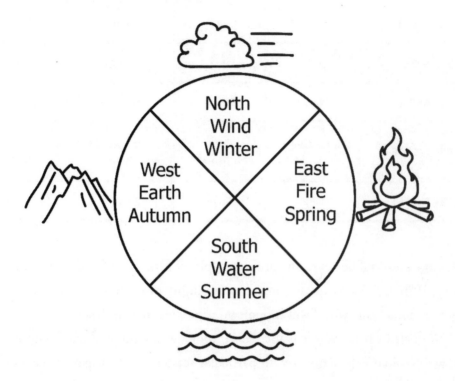

In the Toltec tradition, life is created by the four elements: fire (*huehueteotl*), water (*tlaloc*), air (*ehecatl*), and earth (*tlalnantzin*). Each of these elements works together, and each is represented in our physical body—from the heat we generate in our blood to the water that gives us life and refreshes us to the air we breathe to the earth that makes up our skin and bones.

Looking at the chart on the next page, it's easy to see how the medicine wheel can be helpful. It can provide perspective in moments of crisis, as well as directional guidance for what steps to take. The wheel points to the cyclical impermanence of all things, as well as the eternal spiral of evolution and growth. The wheel is an emblem of all the elements together and is connected to

DIRECTION	North	East	South	West
ELEMENT	Air	Fire	Water	Earth
COLOR	White	Red	Yellow	Black
SEASON	Winter	Spring	Summer	Fall
LIFE STAGE	Elder/Teacher of Teachers	Child/ Participant	Adolescent / Student	Adult / Teacher
ASPECT OF SELF	Mind	Spirit	Emotion	Body

the most powerful healer in the universe—planet earth, and her divine mother energy. When you are experiencing illness or injury or mental suffering, returning to the medicine wheel will support your progress toward healing.

Animals fit into the medicine wheel, too, and are often aligned with one or two dominant elements or with particular seasons or life stages. In the next section of this book, you can feel into these connections for yourself as you read about each animal and see what makes the most sense to you. As you understand more about the medicine wheel and how to place animals within it, you will quickly begin to uncover new insights and lessons from the animal world. Each quadrant has particular strengths and weaknesses, and these relate back to the specific lessons of the animals for you.

I encourage you to call on your intuition and imagination here. It's easy to see how most birds and flying insects belong to the element of air, while two- and four-legged creatures are a part of earth, and fish and other ocean animals belong to water. Many cultures associate reptiles with fire because they often live in hot desert climates and rely on the heat of the sun to warm their blood.

Some connections may feel less obvious or common but will make a lot of sense to you. Remember, these relationships and correspondences are *teaching tools*; they are designed to assist you in your own journey by prompting you to ask certain questions about your strengths, weaknesses, agreements, attachments, and points of healing. They are not meant to be literal and are never set in stone. Go with your instincts; books and teachings like this one are important guides, but you will learn even more by supplementing with your own intuition.

Let's looks at each quadrant of the medicine wheel and explore some of the animals we might find there.

Air (ehecatl)

Air is associated with thought and the mind. Intellect, communication, language, reasoning, and philosophy all belong in this quadrant of the medicine wheel, where the strong, clean winds of winter blow over the barren landscapes and a person can see for many miles over the frozen ground. The color of this quadrant is white, the hue of snow or a blank piece of paper. We can think of air bringing clarity, just as a great wind blows away cobwebs and debris.

Air is the realm of the birds, among them the great raptors who soar high in an empty sky on a clear day, looking down. Hawks and eagles are well-known for their amazing eyesight and incredible hunting abilities. The smallest sparrow can be found meticulously searching the ground for every last crumb of food. Flocks of birds can fly and spin and stay together in complex and responsive patterns.

Beyond birds, we might think of the elemental air qualities of the bat, another winged creature whose unique gift for clarity comes from its use of echolocation, which allows bats to "see" in the dark. I know personally how powerful the teaching of the bat can be. After an illness left me unable to see for a time as a child, the bat became one of my personal power animals and taught me not only how to "see" by using my other senses but also how to be strong and resourceful in times of darkness—how to navigate a difficult time in my life both literally and emotionally.

Think for a moment about the element of air. It can take the form of a gentle breeze or a powerful tornado or hurricane. Likewise, think of what might happen if we had no air at all. If you were to pause your breath for a moment at the very end of an exhale, you'd feel a stirring in the body, ready to take in new air. Air is vital to life. The animals of air, even those that appear delicate and ephemeral like the butterfly, have powerful lessons to share.

Fire (huehueteotl)

Fire is the element of spirit, an aspect of ourselves we often don't understand. This part of the medicine wheel is aligned with the color red—the hue of energy and creativity—as well as with the life-giving sun, which rises in the east, and with the return of new life in the spring as the sun warms the earth again. In this way fire also symbolizes childhood, new beginnings, and new identities or aspects of ourselves.

Fire is also an energizing catalyst in the natural world. The giant sequoia, for example, cannot release its seeds without the powerful heat generated in a forest fire. Traditional medicine understands that the destructive power of fire is entwined with new growth and new possibility. Fire animals command great respect. When we understand them, we can set aside fear and work with their unique powers. Think of the snake: often misunderstood and feared, in truth it is closely aligned with healing, transformation, and sexual power.

Fire also holds an important place in ritual and ceremony, in ways that range from lighting candles of remembrance to clearing space energetically or letting go of what we no longer need. We might think of fire as that eternal flame that exists within us all—an expression of our life force. We can choose how we tend that flame and how we share it with the world. Fire animals such as lizards or even the mythical phoenix can help us remember how to do this.

Water (tlaloc)

Water is the element of emotion, flow, and adaptability. Healing, change, and movement are all a part of this quadrant of the medicine wheel, which is associated with the color yellow. Water is life, cycling through the earth without ceasing, falling down from rain clouds and bubbling up from underground springs. Movement and flow keep water fresh and oxygenated; when water is blocked, it can stagnate and collect debris. Water is always critical to life, but in the hot dry summertime it becomes even more of a precious gift.

The vast oceans that dominate our planet are home to thousands and thousands of species of fish, mammals like whales and dolphins, crustaceans, jellyfish, and more. Despite the many thousands of years we've been living on this planet, we have hardly ventured into the reaches of the sea, and new species are being uncovered all the time. Consider how the same might be said of our inner selves and our emotional lives. We have an ocean inside us of untapped potential, dreams, imagined landscapes, and stories. By partnering with the animals who inhabit the water, we can learn how to dive deep into our own potential.

Another important aspect of water is its connection to youth or adolescence—a time of change, adaptation, exponential growth, new learning, social connection, adventurous spirit, and play. Water animals can inspire us to reconnect with these qualities in ourselves no matter where we are in our life's journey.

Earth (tlalnantzin)

As the sun falls each day, it comes to rest in the blanket of the earth. This quadrant of the medicine wheel represents adulthood, a time when we have enough knowledge and experience to become teachers (though we never stop learning). This part of the medicine wheel brings abundance in the form of the fall harvest and reminds us to build up our stores and protect ourselves and our families for the winter months ahead. The color of this quadrant is black, which evokes the clear night sky overhead as well as the deep nourishing soil under our feet. It also brings to mind death and the afterlife, as the body returns to earth, its home.

Animals aligned with the earth include many four-legged creatures such as bison, deer, and elephants. It also includes the burrowing creatures who store food and whose wisdom reminds us that small, earnest actions can have a big impact over time. These animals remind us that we are of the earth—the minerals in rock and soil make up an important part of who we are. It is impossible to feel separate from the earth when we tap into the particular wisdom of this part of the medicine wheel. Earth knowledge helps us all claim responsibility for cocreating the Dream of the Planet. These animals remind us that we are not alone. We are all siblings, children of Mother Earth.

Your Power Animals

Throughout your lifetime, you may feel drawn to working with a few particular animals, which you might think of as your personal power animals. These special companions hold meaning for you and travel with you on your journey. You can return to them again and again for inspiration and guidance. My power animals are the bat, the rattlesnake, and the jaguar.

I already mentioned my connection to the bat, which helped me understand a new way of seeing at a time when I was temporarily blinded due to illness. Today, bat medicine reminds me that when I feel lost or can't see something clearly, I can bypass my mind and follow my heart and intuition instead. The bat has given me a way to home in on my own inner guidance while being blind to whatever outside glimmers might distract or tempt me.

I am also connected to the rattlesnake. As babies, rattlesnakes cannot control their venom, and at one time I also was that way with my emotional venom. When I was upset, I would "bite" whoever came near me, no matter what their intentions, and I would release all my venom at once. But I matured as a rattlesnake does; I became aware of my venom and learned to control it.

My third spirit animal is the jaguar. The jaguar hunts by stalking and embodies action in the moment. The jaguar holds intent and force and power. I call on the spirit of the jaguar when I need to move forward, when my doubts and fears would rather keep me locked up and passive. When I call on this incredibly powerful animal, I remind myself that I am powerful with my intent and can manifest my own desires, dreams, and goals if I take the actions required.

Everyone is capable of establishing this special relationship with a power animal. You may already have an animal or two or three that you know are an important part of your life or that seem to appear regularly in your dreams or in everyday life. Some people developed an interest in a specific animal as a child or receive regular gifts related to an animal. These may be signs that you have subconsciously chosen your spirit animals. However, don't feel bound to pick something that others associate with you. Leave room to be drawn to a particular animal or an attribute you'd like to cultivate, regardless of what others may think. This is your journey.

At the end of this chapter, you will find an exercise to guide you in choosing your own power animals.

Personal Altar and Medicine Bag

Personal altars and medicine bags are ancient tools used by shamans to help bring inner intentions into the physical world. An altar can take many forms, but at its core it is an area dedicated to special objects and images that guide one's journey. Indoors or outdoors, tiny or sprawling, altars can engage all of the senses through color, texture, and smell, and can also incorporate elements of water, air, earth, and fire. Power animals can find their place here too, in the form of pictures or drawings, shells, bits of feather, fur, or bone.

Likewise, the medicine bag can provide a physical anchor for spiritual focus. Usually a small pouch made of leather, medicine bags have been crafted and worn by countless people as they have sought awakening. One might carry a prayer, sticks, bones, rocks, feathers, or shells inside. It might contain an object that is the symbol of a vision, a piece of nature from a meaningful place, or a talisman of a power animal. Whatever items the medicine bag contains, they are all physical representations to guide the inner journey of the wearer.

Consider incorporating power animals into your existing altar or medicine bag or including animal wisdom in any new spaces you create. One of the most powerful ways to work with animals is through rituals connected to these items.

Key Tools for Working with Power Animals

Most of this book is devoted to information about power animals, listed one by one. I hope the entries will be engaging, but it's even more important that they are only the beginning of your experience with animal wisdom. For that reason, I want to spend some time laying out how to work with power animals. Again, I want to emphasize that this is your own personal journey. Animal medicine is meant to be practiced with creative intention by each shaman individually, for a shaman follows his or her own deep inner truth—not the authority or tradition of others for their own sake. You get to choose how to work with these animals in the way that best serves your journey toward understanding and living within the true nature of the universe. You get to create and live your own personal beautiful dream, healing yourself and being held by the unconditional love that surrounds us at all times, whether our busy minds allow us to see it or not.

To that end, here are a few of the powerful ways you can work with animals to start you on your journey or add to your existing practices.

Animal Protectors and Guides

One way to work with the animals in this book or others that come into your life is to call on their particular attributes in a way related to a certain time or experience you are having. One simple example comes from a friend of mine, who put a little stuffed bear into her daughter's bag for the first day of kindergarten.

The girl felt she had the courage of the bear walking with her as she set out on her new adventure at school. An animal might be called upon as a protector and guide for a difficult journey or task, reminding us to be clear-eyed like the eagle or playful like the otter.

It's important to note that we should be careful of those who have created and used stories about animal behavior or meaning to manipulate other humans. This is part of domestication. Animal stories sometimes evoke superstition and fear, so we can have great respect for the teachings of the animal world and at the same time investigate certain beliefs or stories about animals by asking, *Is this true for me?* The animal that brings comfort to one person may inspire unhelpful superstition in another. It is our job to stay aware and keep checking in with ourselves.

Being Present in Reality

I have four little dogs at home, and one thing I love is that no matter what challenges I am experiencing in my Personal Dream, when I walk in the front door they are always happy to see me. They share their love with me no matter what. Every time I experience this, I am reminded of this profound difference between humans and the rest of the animal world.

As mentioned earlier, humans have a mind that is constantly dreaming, and for so many of those who live their lives unconsciously, the mind overflows with regrets of the past, fears of the future, or negative judgments of the present. Unlike humans, animals live only in the present moment. They don't tell stories to themselves about how they are not good enough or worry that they might never find true love. So even though they may experience challenges and a range of emotions, animals don't create problems for themselves via a dreaming mind. They enjoy a closer relationship to the reality of the present moment than most humans. Working with any animal can help renew this connection to reality for us too.

Tuning In to the Natural World

When we think of animal wisdom, we can draw on images of iconic wild animals like the bobcat, coyote, eagle, or bear. But even daily sightings and interactions with local animals and our pets provide countless insights. When we become observers of animals or imagine observing our world as an animal does, it can remind us to live in the moment in a powerful way. This is one of the reasons that animals figure so strongly in shamanic storytelling. By emphasizing an animal's attributes through the art of story, we can reveal the importance of their unique gifts. We can explore the potential of adopting these gifts in pursuit of creating our own dream.

Seeing a spider weave a web in the corner of a windowsill, watching a squirrel diligently bury food in the park, or listening to the call and response of the birds in your area are all ways to tune in to the natural world, which is always unfolding in the present moment. The idea of synchronicity can also help us access these teachings. When we open up to the natural world, we may begin to notice certain patterns or coincidences in animal sightings that can provide new tools. Seeing a cartoon fox on TV or noticing a little dog curled up like a fox, for example, can remind you to call on the cunning of the fox when you need it.

We can also be inspired by animal stories, behaviors, and attributes. Whether they come to us in waking hours or when we dream, the mysteries of animals excite the human imagination. Our imagination is one of our most powerful gifts for healing ourselves and manifesting our heart's desire. Animals bring us into alignment with our imaginative powers.

Finally, animals can bring forward gratitude for the natural world and our place in it. You might already have a practice of gratitude for the gifts of animals that provide what we eat or the clothes we wear (though refusing both of these can also be a choice based in gratitude and respect). Beyond that, we can live in gratitude for a multitude of physical and spiritual gifts from the animal world and for the reminder that we are part of nature too—it could be no other way.

Including Power Animals in Ritual

Rituals aid your journey of awakening from your individual dream and the collective Dream of the Planet, so that you can more readily heal and be healed of your addiction to suffering.

When I speak of ritual in this way, I don't mean religious practices, though if those are part of your shamanic journey that can be wonderful too. This is about using ritual to make manifest our inward desires in the physical world. This can take so many forms, but you will know what's right for you. Whether it's praying, dancing, sitting in quiet contemplation, or performing sacred ceremonies with your altar or medicine bag, ritual is a way to further your practice, wherever you currently stand on your journey. Consider bringing animal wisdom into your current rituals and allowing their powerful energy to help you on your path.

In the same way, there are many instances when it is helpful to work with animals in a concrete way. Sometimes, we can get attached to an idea or singular "meaning" of an animal. This often comes from our own domestication or our need for certainty. The lion is "king of the jungle"; elephants "never forget." To counter this, I encourage you to work with animals in ritual in concrete ways. For example, if you dream of a whale, resist deciding what this "means." Instead, you might locate a tiny engraving of a whale and carry it around with you. Then, stay curious and open about what comes up. You might add a photograph of a whale tail to your altar and meditate with this image in your mind's eye, gently setting aside any preconceived notions about what message or meaning the animal holds for you. Working in this way, you allow deeper animal wisdom to surface in your life in ways you might not expect.

Animal Families

I want to note that the list of animals in this book is by no means exhaustive or complete. I hope you will be inspired to make your own additions, so with each entry I have included a collection of other related animals. I encourage you to explore any variations within closely related animals and see what resonates best for you. For example, the lion, the tiger, and the jaguar reflect many of the same qualities; they have simply taken on different physical forms depending on the habitat in which they live. Even though they have some physiological and behavioral differences, the spirit energy—the animal medicine—of each of these magnificent creatures is largely the same. Often these variations will seem to belong in different parts of the medicine wheel or in unique relationships to what the elements represent. For example, the river otter may help you see the emotional element of water as a connected network, always flowing between people and places. Or you might be more drawn to the sea otter, who frolics and thrives in the emotional landscape of the wide, mysterious ocean. You may choose one over the other depending on where you are in the world, or you may invite the energy of one to help you out of personal preference.

I have included reference to similar animals where applicable in Part Two; "related animals" refers to those animals not already discussed in this book but that have similar qualities, and animals already listed in this book that you may want to review in addition to a given entry are included under "see also."

In some cases, you may find that the animals under "related animals" or "see also" bear no scientific relationship to one another. This may cause a moment of confusion, but even though they may seem unrelated at first, they are included due to their mythological, energetic, or spiritual connection. This is the case for example with the trickster figures included here, which appear in various cultures across the world: the crow, the fox, the rabbit, the coyote, and the spider—all important contributions. Other animals may share an energy—a characteristic or signature trait—that links them together beyond appearances on the surface. If a related animal strikes you as confusing, you may find it a powerful exercise to sit for a while with that pairing and listen for any intuitive hints as to why they may be linked. You may even discover through such an exercise that you make entirely new associations between animals you hadn't considered before, which will only enhance your work with these complex and amazing beings.

Power Animal Exercises

The following exercises offer a variety of opportunities to strengthen your connection to the diversity of animal life and the wealth of teachings they offer. As you read through these, note any exercises you feel drawn to over others; those you find particularly compelling are usually the best places to begin. Always trust your intuition!

Observing the Animal World

Taking time to observe animals is a great gift and can teach us so much. You can observe animals at any time, from those you come into physical contact with to the animals you can find in the vast libraries of raw footage online that features animals from all over the world. It could be the insect that lands on your arm, a pigeon on the sidewalk, or a family of meerkats at the zoo. All animals have something to teach if we're willing to learn. In any case, as you observe, you might want to keep a journal handy to make a note of any moments that have a particular effect on you in a physical, emotional, or spiritual way.

Begin by settling into your space. Let go of any past fears or anxieties. Let your mind drop into a receptive, watchful state. Take a deep breath. If you're outside, you may wish to spend some time with your eyes closed, imagining yourself to be a tree, rock, or other part of the landscape. This helps to send an energetic message to the animals in the area that you are a friendly observer only and not a threat.

As you observe an animal, see if you can bring to mind any associations you may already have with that creature. There may be mythological, religious, or cultural stories built over generations of animal observation that can tell us something about the gifts these animals have offered to our ancestors, and which may still have meaning for us today.

Consider how these gifts may help you in your personal life and whether or not they're true for you. How might your inner self, your healing journey, and your community benefit from the swift dart of the garter snake, the unceasing song of the cicada, or the conserving hibernation of the hedgehog or the bear?

Make it a point in all of your observations to note the presence and grace that each animal has within them, without the dreaming mind and its addiction to suffering.

Once you have spent some time in conscious observation with an animal and have considered the gifts it offers, you may wish to go further and imagine that you are able to move your consciousness into its body and see through its eyes. What does the world look like from this perspective? Notice the moment-to-moment aliveness to the present circumstances without getting tripped up in the past or future. Step into the mind of the animal you are watching. That idea may seem strange, that you can place your own mind inside another being, but in Toltec shamanism we don't believe consciousness is confined to the mind or body. That is to say, it's not localized in the brain. This allows the shaman to "reach out" with their consciousness and communicate with the living world in a more profound way, enabling them to see through the eyes of our brother and sister animals, as well as plants, rivers, mountains, and the planet.

When your observations come to a close, say a short thank you to the animal for the lessons it has to teach, and for spending time with you that day. You may want to leave a small offering of seeds or other food as a way to express your gratitude. Take some time to write your observations and notes in your journal.

Choosing Your Power Animals

The personal power animals you choose don't have to be set in stone. Things can always evolve. However, I find that dedicating some time and attention to the process of choosing three special animals for yourself can reveal a lot about where you are now and how animals can be an important part of your journey of healing and presence.

To begin this practice, settle into a quiet place and do a silent meditation for at least five minutes, but more if you feel so moved. Let your mind release any busy thoughts and focus on your breath. Feel your connection to each of the four elements. Notice where your body touches the ground and feel the energy that rises up from the earth into you. Tune in to any warmth in your body and place one hand on your chest to feel the beating of your heart. Feeling the sensations of your breath, rest your other hand on your belly and notice it rise and fall. Place your awareness on your skin and the quality of the air on it. Finally, imagine that you are a vessel, and that an imaginary rain is falling from above, filling you up and quenching and revitalizing every cell of your body.

When you feel calm and relaxed, read the following prayer out loud:

Animal spirits, allies and guides,
Friends of feather, fur, and claw,
I open my heart and seek your wisdom.
Teachers of the living world,
You are welcome here.

When your prayer is complete, write down any animals that enter into your mind. I encourage you to do this all at once without limiting or editing your thoughts—animals may come through that you don't expect. Then review your list and write down all the qualities each animal represents for you. Here are a few examples to get you started:

Butterfly: Nurturing, Transformative, Inspiring

Cat: Independent, Curious, Mysterious

Eagle: Powerful/Strong, Brave, Authoritative/Decisive

Earthworm: Humble, Hands-on, In It for the Long Haul

Elephant: Kind/Empathetic, Family-oriented, Dignified/Rarefied

Horse: Free/Balanced/Swift, Cooperative, Proud/Noble

Komodo Dragon: Primal, Imaginative, Ancient

Rabbit: Clever, Fertile, Discreet

Rattlesnake: Respected, Restrained, Reserved

Shark: Energetic, Driven, Explorative

Squirrel: Curious/Determined, Ready, Grounded

Turtle: Wise, Prepared, Patient/Trusting

Whale: Contemplative/Peaceful, Emotional, Communicative

Remember, the qualities listed here are what these animals represent to me—but what's important is what the animals represent to *you*. The path of the shaman is about following your own truth, and yours will be different from mine.

After you've made your list, contemplate each animal and its attributes, and then pick three that have traits you currently see or want to cultivate within yourself.

After you have made your selections, close the ceremony by thanking the animals for coming to you in this way. Over the next few days, find a symbol representing each of your three animals for your personal altar or medicine bag. This could be a feather, some of the animal's fur, a small statue, or even a photo of the animal. Notice any synchronicities or animal visitations.

Calling On the Spirit of a Power Animal to Help

One simple way to practice working with power animals is to call on them for help. What do you want? What do you need?

Perhaps you would like to feel more focused on a task you need to finish. Why not call on the gifts of the woodpecker, who listens intently for its quarry and then bangs away until it gets inside to eat?

Maybe you are longing to make your space more comfortable and inviting. Why not call on your feathered power animal to help with nesting or a small mammal to make a sweet and cozy burrow?

Perhaps you need boldness. You can ask for help from a powerful hunter.

Or rest, and you can call on some languid feline help as you curl up for a nap.

If you are struggling to make a big change in your life, call on the power of the butterfly to transform.

If you are hoping to expand your family, ask the rabbit for her blessings.

Start calling in your spirit animals when you need their gifts to manifest during your day or for a long-term project or relationship. You can do this in any number of ways, so experiment with what feels right to you.

It might be a phrase such as, "Sister dolphin, will you help me find time to play today?" or "Earthworm, please guide me in making fertilizer from the dung heaped in front of me."

It also doesn't have to be this literal. You could remind yourself of your animal's power and ask for their help through movement, such as taking a few cat-like steps, bobbing up and down like a bird, or closing your eyes and spreading your "wings" to call on the power of the bird family. Likewise, you might hum a tune or imitate an animal noise to call in help from the natural world.

Finally, you don't have to invoke the power of an animal for any specific request or purpose at all. You can simply choose to move through your day with a little more grasshopper energy or with the curiosity and agility of a spider monkey.

After a month or two of regularly calling on your spirit animals, return to your list and write down any new qualities you have discovered in your time working with them.

Stalking the Self: A Journey with Your Spirit Animal

For this exercise, you'll focus on one animal spirit only. To start, find a safe, comfortable space where you can be free from interruption for at least thirty minutes. Sit in a comfortable chair with your feet flat on the ground, connecting you to Mother Earth.

Center yourself by taking a few deep, calming breaths. Let go of any anxieties about the future or worries from the past—there is only you in this space at this perfect time.

Close your eyes, and picture in your mind your spirit animal. If you have an established way of contacting your animal, such as going to a specific place in the inner world to meet them, please do so. When I say *inner world*, I mean whatever version of your imaginative consciousness comes up for you in meditation, prayer, visualization, or a dream state. In this space, see your animal in front of you and be filled with the joy and peace of being in the presence of this powerful, loving ally.

Look into the eyes of your spirit animal—notice how they differ from your human eyes. They may be piercing, like the eyes of a bird of prey, or deep liquid pools like those of an otter. See them move toward you until their eyes are right in front of you. Now imagine you close your eyes in the inner world, and when you open them, you are no longer looking at the eyes of your spirit animal; you are looking through them. Look around at the inner world through the eyes of this amazing creature. What is it like to see with the eyes of your spirit animal? What do you notice that you may not have noticed before? Explore the landscape that fills the inner mind as you travel in your animal's consciousness, whether it's jungle, desert, ocean, or grassy backyard.

You may also wish to view a part of your human life with the eyes of your spirit animal. This can be a very powerful experience. Think of a time and place in your life you would like to visit; this could be a happy occasion or a difficult time. What does looking at this event through the eyes of your animal reveal to you? What qualities does your animal offer that you might not have had on your own? (Note: If you become too emotionally involved in the scene, you may realize that you are no longer seeing through the eyes of your spirit animal. Simply take some deep, cleansing breaths and return to your animal.)

Revisiting your human experience in the body of your spirit animal allows you to do what some shamans call *stalking the self*, and it can lead to powerful revelations and personal healing. Know that in every moment, you are protected by your spirit animal. Together with this ally you can guide yourself out of your own negative stories and see the truth of your life.

When you are ready, close your eyes in the inner world, and when you open them, you will be seeing through your own eyes once again and looking into the face of your beloved friend. Thank them for their help and guidance, and ask them if there are any additional messages for you at this time. Close your eyes once again.

Once you have said goodbye, return to your body in the living world. Take several deep breaths and stretch your arms and legs. Wiggle your toes and fingers. When ready, open your eyes and return completely to this space at this time.

I recommend that you spend some time immediately after this exercise recording your experiences in a journal so you can be sure to capture the details and return to them later for further reflection.

As always, I encourage you to explore your own intuitive callings as you build your dialogue with one or several different beings. Take time to consider what methods fit you best, and in what way they might become a seamless part of your practice as a whole. If you are dedicated to journaling and the written word, your work with your power animals may be more focused on writing; whereas others may be more drawn to creating and performing personal rituals, meditation and visualization, drawing, or singing. Find the path that helps you incorporate the teachings of the animals in the most potent and transformational process for you.

In the next section you'll find an in-depth reference guide to specific animals with notes on their attributes, teachings to consider when encountering them (whether symbolically or physically in the natural world), and suggested practices and prayers for inviting their energy into your life.

PART TWO

RESOURCE GUIDE TO ANIMALS

The following pages are filled with animal information and inspiration and are meant to be used in any way you like. Start at the beginning or flip through and read an entry at random. Look up an animal you see in the world or that comes to you in a dream. Return to your three power animals and make notes in the margins or in your journal. Remember, you may not know why you are drawn to a certain animal or what guidance it may be offering you. Keep connecting to what you feel inside. When you read about an animal, do you feel a tugging in your solar plexus (the center of your torso just below your breastbone)? Do you have the desire to put the book down and do more research or find a way to observe the animal more closely? Go with your instincts!

Each entry includes some suggested practices and a prayer for calling the powers of the animal to you in times of need, but don't hesitate to write your own. Words that come from your own heart and personal connection will tie your intentions to the power of the animals in even stronger ways. Each entry also includes some examples of animals with similar medicine, as well as references to the animal's place in the medicine wheel, which often spans two quadrants and is also open for your own shamanic interpretation.

Remember that you may be drawn to different animals at different times of your life, and even on different days or at different times of day. Your three main power animals will always travel with you, but you may also need to call upon others from time to time; for example, the teachings of the wolf to work with others and tackle a particularly elusive project or the rattlesnake to help you be clear about your boundaries.

A journal can be a great resource during this process as well. If you feel called by an animal in the following pages (or one not listed here), spend some time writing about them in your notebook. If possible, go to a place where you may be able to safely observe one, either in the wild or at a local animal sanctuary, and journal about your experiences there. Take notes on the animal's behavior. How does it move? How does it rest? How does it interact with its surroundings?

Consider including sketches with your descriptions. You don't have to be a professional artist—this is a skill that anyone can learn, practice, and enjoy— and this detailed observation brings us into closer contact with power animals. Try to release any negative self-judgment about your abilities and enjoy the process of learning.

Movement and music can also enrich your spiritual exploration of the animal world. There are several martial arts and dance practices that mirror and incorporate animals. From the quality of certain motions to the mindset of animals, these movement practices can be powerful ways to tap into animal medicine and expand our practice. Finally, I encourage you to draw on the power of sound and music in this area. From pop lyrics to natural soundscapes to howling like a coyote on a full moon, let yourself explore the sonic aspects of animal medicine.

A note on encountering power animals: In the entries below, you will see teachings to remember when you encounter an animal. Keep in mind that this may not be a literal encounter with a physical animal. Encounters may take the form of dream animals, cultural images, art, or literary references. For example, you may suddenly notice that you've seen more than a few references to bears in the last few weeks: on a necklace of a friend, then on the cover of a book, then in a nature documentary. Then you recall that you had a dream a few weeks ago where an enormous black bear walked past your living room window. This is the living world speaking to you through signs, dreams, and intuition. Even one sign at just the right moment can have meaning. These are legitimate power animal encounters, even if you do not run into a physical bear in the wild.

ALLIGATOR

See also: Komodo Dragon, Turtle

Related animals: crocodile, dinosaur, lizard

Elements: water and earth

- Powerful and confident
- Protective
- Observant

Teachings to Remember When Encountering Alligators

We associate alligators and their close cousins crocodiles with territorial strength and aggression. They are armored up in a thick, scaly hide, and they can move with great stealth and speed in water and on land alike. Their ferociously strong jaws and powerful tails can kill prey or adversaries in a single bite or blow. For all their ferocity, however, alligators reveal powerful teachings about the wisdom of our instinctual emotional body.

Alligators are ancient creatures and spend much of their life in the water, the element of emotion. These animals cut a graceful path through murky waters, relying on their physical adaptations and primal instincts to survive. Likewise, we can be guided by our own primal, instinctual, and ancient emotional selves. When we encounter physical danger or psychological provocation, the primordial, powerful being within us leaps into action. Imagine what we can accomplish when we harness this energy.

In your mind's eye, picture an alligator submerged in water, with only its eyes peeking above the surface. Like the alligator, we can remain immersed in powerful emotions without losing our ability to cultivate observation and awareness. This allows us to remain balanced—supported and nourished by our feelings but not overwhelmed by them.

The ancient Egyptians worshipped a crocodile-headed god called Sobek, whose aggressiveness was prized by pharaohs. In addition, Sobek's qualities of fierce protection and nurturing were emulated by rulers intent on providing for their people and the welfare of their land. Alligators are territorial creatures and will defend their young. We can learn from their example how to set boundaries, care for our home, and watch over what is important to us.

Questions to Consider

- Do you feel you know your own emotional strength, or does it take you by surprise? Consider your relationship to personal power and how your emotions support or hinder it.

- How do you protect what you cherish most?

- Do you leap into action or consider the consequences first? If you take a few extra moments to observe and reflect, how might this affect your actions?

Calling the Spirit of the Alligator

Your instinctive self or your emotional body, sometimes called the "lizard brain," is the most ancient part of your nervous system, the part of you that has been passed along, unchanged, from earliest human evolution. In every moment, this primal being within you communicates and responds, most often through your body and your instinctual reactions to your environment. Sometimes it overwhelms you without warning, such as in the "fight, flight, or freeze" responses. When we acknowledge and befriend this part of ourselves, we can incorporate it into our daily lives in a healthy way.

Like the alligator floating in the green waters of the swamp or the river, we can tap into our primordial gifts of observation and emotional expression through simple meditation exercises, which become even more powerful through regular practice.

Find a spot where you will be uninterrupted for at least twenty minutes and move into a comfortable position. This can be done sitting, standing, or lying down. Take several deep breaths, allowing your muscles to relax. Begin by bringing your awareness to your toes, sensing where they are and how they feel right now. They might feel toasty warm, or they may be cramped in your shoes. No need to do anything about these sensations, just be aware of them. Next, move your awareness up into your feet and do the same.

Slowly and with care, move your attention up your body, noting the sensations as you go. If any emotions come up for you while you do this, make a note of them, especially how they feel in your physical body. Is there a bit of anxiety gnawing at your stomach? A warm feeling of contentment in your solar plexus? Or impatience manifesting as tingling vibration in your hands and feet? Name these emotions to yourself, without feeling any need to "fix" or "change" them.

When you're finished, allow yourself to get up slowly and stretch. Say a small prayer, silently or aloud, thanking your ancient instinctive self for its gifts.

A Prayer for Alligator Energy

Prehistoric and powerful alligator
Drifting through green and fertile waters
Help me to own my strength, my potency,
Guide me toward a deeper emotional awareness,
And help me be a nurturing protector of all that I love.

ANT

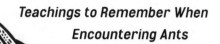

Teachings to Remember When Encountering Ants

Wandering alone, the lowly ant may seem small and insignificant, vulnerable to attack or inadvertently being smushed underfoot. But when we consider the facts that ants never live alone, can be found on nearly every continent, and number in the quadrillions, we can see the power of this creature in a different light. Some ant colonies operate with a hive mind as a single superorganism, capable of building bridges or rafts with their bodies to keep the hive going. They are an ancient species, having been on earth since the age of the dinosaurs. And there is evidence that not only are they hunter-gatherers, but some ant species cultivate aphids and farm certain kinds of fungus in their nests. They are also one of the only non-mammals to have demonstrated an ability to teach and learn.

See also: Bee

Related animals: termite, wasp

Elements: earth and fire

- Constructive
- Organized
- Prepared and productive

Ants build and populate huge colonies, cooperating not only with other ants but with other species of plants and animals as well. Ants have all kinds of relationships with other insects and plants, often mutually beneficial. And while we tend to think of ants as pests, such as the invasive fire ant with its painful sting or the leaf-cutter that can decimate foliage and fruit on a tree overnight, there are in fact a number of ways in which human beings benefit from an interdependent relationship with ants. For example, ants aerate soil and provide natural pest control in some parts of the world.

Moreover, it seems important to note that animals and their spiritual medicine do not exist for human benefit or gain. They belong to themselves. I hold this view even of pets, who cannot be truly owned—we only live alongside them in collaboration. The ant does not care whether or not humans understand or have "proven" the existence of its special attributes. It will carry on working, feeding, building, foraging, and tending. I take this as an excellent reminder that my rational knowledge of animal medicine is not what makes it powerful. The spirit of the animal holds its own power, as I hold mine. My own healing journey and ceremonial practices are enriched by my curiosity and knowledge, and I consider it a great privilege to seek out the lessons offered by the natural world.

In fact, the more we learn about our world, the stronger and more resilient we will become as fully engaged participants in the living world. This is true for all life—there are so many connections between living creatures, more than we could ever learn or map. This is a humbling, great gift.

Ants are often portrayed in folklore as busy, industrious creatures. The famous Aesop fable, "The Ant and the Grasshopper," for example, pits the grasshopper, who lives only for the moment and doesn't make any future plans, preferring to sing all summer, against the hardworking ants, who try to make the grasshopper understand that winter will come and he should be prepared. While today we might argue that the value of the grasshopper's song is equal to the hard work of an ant, there are times when we too need to rally our energy and work cooperatively with others to help better our future.

Questions to Consider

- Do you feel comfortable asking for help, or would you rather manage alone? How might working with a community help you accomplish greater goals?

- What are some ways you can better equip yourself and your community for the future? Can you plant a garden, share resources, or create a local neighborhood network?

- What have you built recently that you are proud of?

Calling the Spirit of the Ant

The ant is a very social creature. While the idea of a hive mind feels like anathema to human individualism, we can learn and appreciate the ant's powerful lessons of cooperation, organization, and hard work. The ant may even whisper in our ear that our sense of individualism is a myth of our own ego. In truth, we are all members of a greater community, whether it's family, fellow artists, animals, or all the earthlings who share this planet. No one stands alone.

At the start of a new project or undertaking, take a moment to close your eyes and envision all the community members who will be involved and working together. This can be a powerful practice to do in a group, standing or sitting in a circle and breathing together, with each person taking a brief mental inventory of all of the fellow hearts, hands, and minds who will set about this task. Don't forget any animal or plant partners, and thank them for their contributions as well.

A Prayer for Ant Energy

Industrious friend ant, builder of great societies,
help us to work together toward a common good;
teach us how to build bridges and listen to each other,
so that together we may thrive even through
difficult times.

BAT

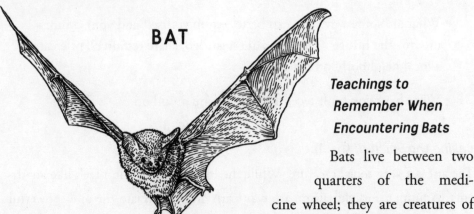

Bats live between two quarters of the medicine wheel; they are creatures of earth and live deep in caves below ground, but they soar through the air on their amazing leathery wings. In some cultures, bats are considered symbols of evil or death, but scratching the surface just a little reveals their incredible diversity and the important role they play in many ecosystems. They pollinate, control insect populations, and much more on every continent with the exception of Antarctica. Some bat species are famous for their echolocation, which allows them to find insects at night and navigate through obstacles at high speeds. This is how they "see" in the dark.

See also: Moth, Owl

Related animals: flying fox, rat

Elements: air and earth

- Sensitive
- Tenacious
- Intuitive

The bat teaches us to follow the resonance of love in our heart and the wisdom of our intuition instead of our eyes. We can call upon the bat to help us in times when we feel emotionally or spiritually lost. The bat helps us tune in to the frequency of our own inner guidance and ignore any noisy, superficial distractions from what is true in our heart.

The bat may also be called upon to help guide you during a dark night of the soul, when it feels as though you may never see the light of dawn ever again. Bats live in darkness without fear. It is their element, and it offers gifts to them that are otherwise unavailable in the light of day. In this way, there are gifts to be discovered even in the darkest of times. The bat helps us find those gifts and be nurtured by them.

Questions to Consider

- What is your intuition telling you today?

- Do you feel like you're "in the dark" in a certain area of your life?

- How could you benefit today by following the love in your heart?

Calling the Spirit of the Bat

To call upon the spirit of the bat, go outside at dusk for the chance to see bats flying overhead. If you live in an area where there is a known bat colony, consider visiting there in the evening and watching as they leave their cave in search of food. You can find footage of this online as well. Listen to the waves of wings pouring out into the open air and notice the ease with which they move into the night and darkness.

Try to find a spot with as little man-made light as possible and close your eyes. Allow your other senses to awaken; the night has many sounds and smells that are otherwise hidden by day.

A Prayer for Bat Energy

Brother bat, night seeker,
flying unafraid through the dark sky,
help me learn to see with my heart.
Teach me how to listen
when all the lights go out.
Brother bat, night seeker!

BEAR

Related animals: kangaroo, koala, panda

Elements: earth

- Powerful
- Protective
- Resourceful and intelligent

Teachings to Remember When Encountering Bears

Can you imagine meeting a bear in a secluded forest clearing? Think of it rearing up on its hind legs, baring its teeth and its razor-sharp claws. For most people this would be a heart-stopping moment—and yet humans from the dawn of time have loved bears. We honor and revere their power, strength, and intelligence, and many cultures have likened bears' shape and intention to that of humans, often imagining that humans could shapeshift into bears for battle, ceremony, or healing purposes. Other people have worshipped bears as gods in animal form.

We love bears so much that we give cuddly, furry replicas of them to our children and write them into beloved stories about characters like Winnie the

Pooh, Paddington Bear, and the Care Bears. We don't do this with other powerful predators like sharks or hawks, so why does the bear hold such power for us?

Like us, bears are smart and resourceful. In some ways, their attributes seem to be superhuman. They are bigger than us, stronger, and even navigate far better than we do. Native healers are said to have learned plant medicine from the bear, who uses it to heal herself. Like us, they use tools, play, grieve their losses, and fiercely protect their young. Bears will put their own lives in jeopardy to save a member of their family.

The spirit of the bear is a popular power animal and an incredible ally for almost any human intention or pursuit. From comfort to protection, from healing to connection with spirit, it's only natural for human beings to feel drawn to such a strong, capable creature. Keep in mind that there is also a wide array of subtler teachings beyond the obvious, and this is for each person to discover on their own. You will know what is right for you. There are messages for us too in the bear's commitment to its family and its way of retreating into sleep in order to conserve energy and live through a difficult, lean time. As you grow a relationship with one of these powerful allies, they will reveal more nuanced, meaningful wisdom over time.

Questions to Consider

- Is there a situation in your life that is causing you stress and would benefit from some profound rest and rejuvenation?

- Are you in need of an ally with superhuman strength and healing powers? What areas in your life could use a burst of bear energy?

Calling the Spirit of the Bear

For animals with the kind of resonant and mythological power of the bear, you might consider tapping into their wisdom through dreamwork. Bears have a metaphorical connection with dreaming because they spend time in hibernation, where they travel through what some shamanic cultures have considered the otherworld—the varied and unpredictable landscape of dream connected to spirit and divinity. Dreams open a powerful gateway to mythic symbolism and the wisdom of our subconscious.

To tap into the power of your dreams, consider keeping a dream journal. Designate a particular journal or notebook just for this purpose, and keep it by the side of your bed with a pen or pencil so you can record your dreams as soon as possible after waking while they're still fresh. What you write down does not need to make sense, and there's no need to spend a lot of time analyzing your dreams. There are certainly dream dictionaries full of particular meanings or interpretations, but those are often other people's stories about dreams. It can be more powerful to follow the stories and patterns of your own dreams and uncover the personal symbology they hold for you.

To invite the spirit of the bear into your sleep, try the practice of dream incubation. Spend a few moments in meditation before bed, calling out to the spirit of the bear to send you a dream or visit you in the otherworld. If you have a question that's been troubling you lately, ask the bear for an answer. Pay special attention to your dreams as you journal about them the next morning, especially if they involved bears or other power animals. This practice calls on the wisdom of your power animals while simultaneously building a passageway to your own powerful subconscious insights.

A Prayer for Bear Energy

Great bear, power and strength,
fierce and tender protector,
be with me as I travel in the land of dream.
Help me find the wisdom within my own mind
to solve the problems in my waking days.

BEE

See also: Ant

See also: Ant

Related animals: termite, wasp

Elements: air

- Lover of beauty
- Community-oriented
- Fertile

*Teachings to Remember
When Encountering Bees*

Bees can be found all over the world, and the honeybee in particular is represented in many different spiritual traditions. All bees are known for the essential pollination service they provide to Mother Earth's plant life, and we share the bounty of the resulting fruit and vegetable harvest. Honeybees are also particularly well-known for their gift for living and working in community, their devotion to acting for the common good, and the geometric harmony of their honeycomb. The fruits of their labor include sweet-smelling beeswax, which has been used in sacred candle making throughout the ages, and of course the delicious honey they produce from the nectar of flowers. Bees remind us of the sweetness of life and the rewards of dedication. There are thousands of species of bees all over the planet, and native bees perform critical functions as pollinators in their particular ecosystems, even if they don't produce honey. For this reason they can be a sign of fertility and procreation or the spreading of metaphorical seeds like ideas and inventions.

Air is of course the element of vision, communication, and clarity, and the bee represents the first two in unique ways. All types of bees have five eyes, two of them compound eyes with many lenses. They can process visual information fifteen times faster than humans, and the three eyes in the center of their foreheads help keep track of the sun for navigation purposes. Bees communicate in fascinating ways as well. For example, when a bee finds a store of nectar while out on her daily explorations, she will communicate its location to the rest of the hive through a special dance called a "waggle dance." Bee medicine can remind us that we also communicate with movement, through gestures, posture, and dance.

In England, there's an ancient tradition called "telling the bees," where great events in a family's life are dutifully carried out into the garden and told to the local hive. In this way, the bees become keepers of history.

Questions to Consider

- Are there any areas in your life that could benefit from working with others?

- Where do you need to see things more clearly?

- Is there a person you need to strengthen your communication with, perhaps in a unique way?

Calling the Spirit of the Bee

We are most likely to find bees in our gardens or nearby parks where there are blossoming flowers. If you go looking for bees, be patient, and if you see bees other than honeybees, this may be a sign for you to learn more about the bumblebees, carpenter bees, mason bees, or other native bees in your area.

Naturally, if you are allergic to bees, use caution. However, if you are not allergic but have a fear or aversion to bees, but feel strangely called to them nonetheless, you may want to explore your fear by considering why they frighten you and what that fear may represent in your life. Is it their sting that frightens you, their unpredictable flying patterns, or the idea of a hive full of backup when they are provoked? How might you work with these fears? What are they telling you?

When you've found an area in which to observe, take your time and open all your senses. See if you can hear the buzz of bee wings as they move from flower to flower. Notice if the bee you are observing has pollen collected on its legs. See if you can smell the flowers blooming in the field and feel the sun warming your face. Allow your heart to open to the joy in that moment—the sweetness of the world.

Consider cultivating a bee-friendly garden. There are many delightful plants that are attractive to human beings as well as offer an opportunity to commune with bees on a regular basis.

A Prayer for Bee Energy

Honeymaker, transforming light
into sweetness. Help me hear the song
of joy in all things.

BEETLE

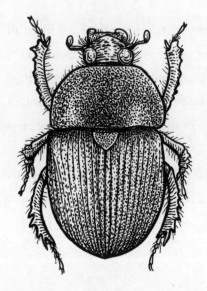

Teachings to Remember When Encountering Beetles

Mythologically speaking, the dung beetle takes first place as the most famous beetle in ancient history. The dung beetle's scientific name, *Scarabaeus sacer*, hints at its significance: the term *sacer* is the Latin word for "sacred" or "revered." The ancient Egyptians considered the dung beetle, also known as the scarab, to be a symbol for Khepri or Khepera, the god of the dawn. Like the dung beetle pushing a ball of dung, Khepera pushes the sun over the horizon each day, bringing light and heat to the world. In this way, Khepera and the scarab that represents him are also a symbol for newness, creativity and becoming, rebirth and regeneration, and moving forward out of darkness into light. The scarab also belongs to the fire element, the element of passion and creativity. The scarab was such a popular symbol that there were countless amulets, jewels, and administrative seals made in the shape of scarabs in ancient Egypt.

It may seem odd to have such reverence for a bug that feeds on waste, but dung beetles are fascinating creatures. They can roll a ball of dung up to ten times their weight and are the only insects known to orient themselves by

Related animals: jewel beetle, june bug, ladybug, weevil

Elements: earth and fire

- Regenerative
- Determined
- Creative

the Milky Way. If you've ever watched footage of a dung beetle rolling its ball across a landscape littered with twigs, leaves, and other obstacles, you know how impressive their perseverance can be! And dung beetles, like every other creature in the web of life, are vital for their waste recycling, seed dispersal, and soil building.

There are around 400,000 species of beetles in the world, and beetles comprise almost 40 percent of all known insects—and 25 percent of all known animal life-forms on the planet. That's a lot of beetles! They are a vast and diverse family with a wide array of colors and sizes. Some beetles have enormous jaws used for fighting, and some have clever camouflage that protects them from predators. Many beetles are black or brown to blend in with the earth, while others are shockingly colorful and iridescent. All beetles have a hard shell that protects their delicate wings beneath.

Questions to Consider

- Are there aspects of your life that you might recycle into something new and nourishing?

- Do you have a long-term project that could use a dose of determination and perseverance? What can you choose to push through and complete?

- What are some of the ways you express your unique spirit in your everyday life? What can you do to feel even more free to be exactly who you are?

Calling the Spirit of the Beetle

Beetles are everywhere, often keeping a low profile. Spend some time getting to know the species that are local to your area. Are you drawn to any in particular? If so, find out more about them and determine a spot where you can observe one uninterrupted in a natural space for a while. Notice the way they trundle along the ground, unfazed by obstacles in their path. If you are drawn to the sacred scarab, you may want to add one to your altar or medicine bag, or wear a piece of jewelry in the form of a scarab.

Another way to connect with the spirit of the beetle is by greeting the dawn. Since time immemorial, humans have found spiritual connection in rising while it's still dark and watching the sun come up from a place of silent reverence. As the sun rises, you may wish to focus your thoughts on who you are becoming in that moment, on that day. What hopes and dreams to you have yet to fulfill? What promise remains unmet within you? Dawn is a perfect time to evaluate your goals and dreams and make plans to accomplish them.

A Prayer for Beetle Energy

Sacred beetle, rising sun,
help me manifest the potential radiance
within me. Lift me up into newness.
As the prism shatters a sunbeam, let the
fire of creativity within me break open into
a thousand shards of color and light.

BISON

Teachings to Remember When Encountering Bison

Millions of bison once roamed North America as the largest mammals on the continent. A keystone species, their life cycles and behaviors have supported the delicate ecology of the plains and grasslands for thousands of years. They are the caretakers of their home and all the creatures who live there. Bison have always played an essential, sacred role in Native American cultures and traditions, providing a wide range of needs to various nations including food, shelter, and clothing.

Related animals: gaur, water buffalo, yak

Element: earth

- Enduring
- Natural
- Steadfast

Despite their tremendous size (they can weigh over a ton), bison can run up to thirty-five or forty miles an hour and jump up to six feet. Though they may look slow and gentle and fluffy from afar, they can be quite dangerous if one isn't respectful of their wild nature and impressive power. One of the lessons the bison teaches is never to assume anything based on appearance.

European settlers hunted bison to the edge of extinction up until the late nineteenth century as part of the genocide and wars of expansion against Native Americans in the American West, killing an estimated thirty to sixty million animals in a few short decades. Today, multiple bison herds live under legal protection, and in 2016 they were declared the national mammal of the United States. In this case, the teaching we receive from the bison is historical as well as mythological and scientific. We have much to learn about living in balance with the other life around us, acting as part of nature rather than separate or above it. Only by honoring the truth of our collective past can we begin to repair damage. Bison medicine reminds us that with collaboration and perseverance, coming back from the brink of ruin is possible.

Of course, the tenacity of the bison themselves accounts for much of the success so far. Bison are notoriously impossible to domesticate. They are unpredictable and refuse to give up their innate wildness, either by training or selective breeding. We humans domesticate other animals and in the Toltec sense of the word we talk about domestication as making agreements based on feedback we receive from family members, media, culture, etc., from an early age. For example, perhaps as a child you loved to draw, but one day another student criticized your work, and that comment became an agreement: "I am not good at drawing." These agreements lead to the domestication of our wild, natural, creative natures. The bison teaches that we can resist and reverse this domestication by ferreting out our agreements, giving them a hard stare with a free wild eye, and refusing to be bound by them any longer.

Questions to Consider

- How have you been domesticated by the messages you heard growing up? What domestications have you accepted that may be holding you back from true personal freedom?

- Is there an assumption you're making about a current situation that needs to be reevaluated?

- Have you felt a nagging sense of negativity lately? What can you do to infuse your outlook with hope?

Calling the Spirit of the Bison

You may have already started the work of freeing yourself from your own domesticating agreements, and if so, the spirit of the bison is a great friend to call on. If you are just beginning this work, you may wish to start with something small. Spend some time meditating or journaling and come up with one dream for your life that you have always harbored but have never been able to move forward with. It may feel like this thing is waiting in the wings for the right moment, that elusive sweet spot when you'll have enough time, talent, money, or whatever else you think you lack. Think about where you may have made an agreement in the past about this dream. When was the seed of that domesticating agreement planted? For instance, maybe your parent stuck with a career they disliked and told you that you would have to do the same to keep food on the table. Or perhaps you tried something you really loved doing, but as a beginner you didn't live up to your own standards, or those of someone else. Chances are that these domesticating influences created a lifetime of beliefs and stories that may not really be true for you. With some work and attention, you can free yourself to embark on a wild new adventure.

If you are drawn to working with the spirit of the bison, one important way to honor their gifts and invite their teachings is to support their rehabilitation and conservation through the U.S. and tribal governing bodies and charitable organizations.

A Prayer for Bison Energy

Powerful teacher bison, fierce and enduring,
help me to free myself from the domesticating
agreements I may have allowed to stifle my inner freedom.
Help me find the courage to let my wild heart
roam free through the wide-open spaces of the world.

BUTTERFLY

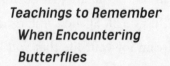

Teachings to Remember When Encountering Butterflies

The delicate and effervescent butterfly has graced our gardens, flitted through our artwork, and settled on our bodies in the form of stunning jewelry for thousands of years. Like living pieces of art, butterflies bring lightness, inspiration, and positivity, and remind us of the staggering ability of all things to change and transform. They embody a paradox of strength and fragility: they are light and breathless, with delicate, paper-thin wings, and eat no solid food, existing solely on the nectar of flowers. Yet some of these airy, ephemeral, sensitive beings, most famously the monarch butterfly, manage to migrate thousands of miles over rough terrain. How could such an animal accomplish so arduous of a journey?

It should come as no surprise that the butterfly has been associated with the soul in many cultures. Ghostlike and ephemeral, they begin life as a grounded being, a caterpillar. In order to complete its total physical transformation, the caterpillar's body dissolves in the chrysalis stage into an amorphous goo, then rearranges, rebuilds, and is reborn into the winged creature we know. Recent

See also: Dragonfly, Hummingbird, Moth

Elements: air and earth

- Nurturing
- Transformative
- Inspiring

studies have found that butterflies "remember" stimulus they experienced in their caterpillar stage—their essence remains throughout this profound transformation.

Some cultures view the butterfly as a symbol for the eternal soul that resides in each of us throughout our lives and beyond death, while others associate the butterfly more with the unbound spirits of the dead. Either way, butterfly wisdom tells a compelling story of inner journeying, change, growth, and transformation. When we encounter a profound shift in our lives—physical, emotional, spiritual, or otherwise—we commune with the spirit of the butterfly.

Transformation is neither easy nor comfortable. No matter how necessary it is, or how delightful and refreshing it feels on the other side of a metamorphosis, going through change can be harrowing. It takes a lot of faith, strength, and vulnerability to dissolve the old and create the new. In that process, we can give ourselves permission to mourn what is passing and ask for help and protection as we make the journey. During these times of soul trial, we can reach out to the spirit of the butterfly to ask for guidance, to help us remember that this great rearranging holds the promise of wings on the other side.

Questions to Consider

- Can you feel a transformation starting to stir in you now? What do you need to bring with you into your cocoon, and what will you leave behind?

- Have you forgotten that anything that will happen in the future is present right now in a seed or larval stage? Can you focus on what you would like to nurture in the present so that you can transform it with intention into the future you desire?

- If you are feeling stuck, can you look for the beauty and lightness around you? The lightest creatures can accomplish the most difficult journeys.

Calling the Spirit of the Butterfly

Cultivate a garden of butterfly-friendly plants such as bee balm, allium, corn-flowers, and zinnias. Most important of all, add plants that caterpillars can munch on. Monarch butterflies can only eat milkweed, for example. A garden like this will also attract native bees and other essential pollinators. My friend has plantings at the end of her walk that welcome scores of monarch butterflies every October as they wing their way south. Her daily walk to the mailbox becomes filled with light and the fluttering of orange wings.

On a spiritual level, you may want to spend some time with the idea that we are always in some phase or another of a great transformation. As you meditate on your soul's journey up to the present, take some time to write in your journal about your experiences from a butterfly perspective. What was it like to be in the caterpillar stage of a particular transformation? What about inside the cocoon? Emerging as a butterfly? How can you prepare yourself for the tumult and potential chaos of this process? Remember that the butterfly can be a potent ally for you and is hardier than it looks. As you reflect on your past transformation, draw small butterflies all around in your notebook, and find a prayer like the one below that resonates with you to call the spirit of the but-terfly to your side for your journey.

A Prayer for Butterfly Energy

Butterfly spirit sister,
little soul who lives on flowers,
bring your breathless beauty into
my heart and alight there, whispering
your wisdom. Teach me how to
hold myself open in this process of transformation,
so that I too may grow wings and fly.

CAT

Teachings to Remember When Encountering Cats

House cats are the only domesticated cat on earth and beloved as pets and companions. Some researchers think that both cats and dogs may have domesticated *themselves*—that is, certain individuals figured out that they enjoyed collaborating with humans, providing rodent control and cuddles to people and getting safety, warmth, food, and affection in return. Yet house cats do retain some of the wildness of their bigger cat cousins. They can nap most of the day away, and then hear a noise or see a movement and go into the kind of full, instinctual mode of the leopard, jaguar, or other great cat hunter. They have little trouble fending for themselves outside the home and can subsist by hunting rodents, birds, and lizards.

See also: Jaguar, Lion

Related animals: bobcat, cougar, lynx, ocelot, panther, serval, tiger

Element: earth

- Independent
- Curious
- Mysterious

The quiet dignity, aloof pride, and exceptional grace of the cat has long captured the imagination of humans. They have the reputation of always being able to land on their feet, and while this is not technically true 100 percent of the time, cats do have a righting reflex that allows them to flip themselves midair and land on their feet most of the time. Metaphorically, the ability to land safe and sound in a time of emotional turbulence or free fall seems like a superpower most of us would be happy to have.

Cats are invoked in the proverbial warning "curiosity killed the cat." They do get into pickles sometimes when they can't help but explore a strange sound, a hole in the ground, or a high-up branch or ledge. Yet the teachings of cats themselves don't discourage us from being curious—the saying more often comes from frustrated humans who don't want to accommodate any changes of plan. The gift of curiosity leads us to all kinds of creative discoveries and reflects a love of learning. Cat curiosity can be paired with the wisdom of balance and caution so that we don't run full tilt into unwanted danger.

Cats seem to hold a special, dignified mystery. Their gliding movement, watchful gaze, and keen instincts have been featured in many myths and legends. For example, the ancient Egyptian cat goddess Bast is the deity of beauty and love. Cats hold a kind of wonder in their very being. When we are around them, we can imagine that anything is possible.

Questions to Consider

- Do you feel off-balance or in emotional free fall? How can you make it right and land on your feet?

- Has your sense of curiosity gotten you into trouble lately? How can you balance curiosity with caution?

- What renews your sense of mystery and beauty in the world?

Calling the Spirit of the Cat

The stunning balance and grace of the cat can serve as an example of how we can juggle our mind, body, and spirit in this life. Working on your physical ability to keep your footing through strengthening and balancing practices and poses in yoga can help you to find the kind of lithe lightness of the cat in the physical realm. For balance in other aspects of your life, consider spending some time in reflection and meditation, or with your journal.

Consider an area of your life that you find out of balance. What does this mean to you? What would this part of your life look like if it were full of grace and poise? How can you imagine moving through this period with the kind of fearless nonchalance of the cat? Whenever you feel like you are out of balance and need a moment to ground and land on your feet, reach out to the wisdom and teachings of the cat. Take a deep breath, lift your head up, and move forward with confidence. You are in full possession of yourself and your life.

A Prayer for Cat Energy

Mysterious, beautiful companion cat,
who moves through the night with grace
and balance, help me to find all the right ways
to land on my feet. Teach me to tap into the
unseen wonder that radiates through the
living world at all times.

CHAMELEON

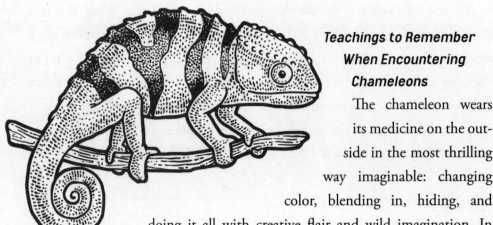

Teachings to Remember When Encountering Chameleons

The chameleon wears its medicine on the outside in the most thrilling way imaginable: changing color, blending in, hiding, and doing it all with creative flair and wild imagination. In addition to this amazing talent, some chameleon species can lash out their enormously long tongues at alarming speeds to capture food, and some have prehensile tails that can grip tree branches as they go. Their eyes can focus independently, which allows the chameleon to look at two different things at the same time.

Related animals: cuttlefish, octopus, pacific tree frog, seahorse

Element: fire

- Creative
- Changeable
- Insightful

This astonishing set of attributes makes the chameleon one of Mother Nature's most delightful and bizarre creatures. Its wisdom is truly unique.

The chameleon sits smack in the middle of the food web—always looking to eat and always working to avoid being eaten. This is basic survival, but it doesn't mean it can't be done in a fabulous way! Meeting our own needs can sometimes feel oppressive or boring. More brown rice? Another workout? Staying within a budget? But we're not locked in to how we meet our needs, either, and rather than feel trapped by them, the chameleon guides us to working outside the box.

There may be all kinds of inventive changes we can make to our own lives that would allow us to open up the passionate, creative parts of ourselves.

This of course requires opening up to different ways of seeing, stepping into our inherent weirdness, widening our perspective, staying flexible, and embracing paradox and chaos with curiosity. It's easy to get stuck in one way of thinking or doing. The secret is that it's easy to get unstuck too. Making up a new joke or a silly dance, playing a game of "the floor is lava!"—these change how you perceive the world, if only for a few moments. The more difficult practice is getting unstuck over and over again and applying what you learn to the larger issues and problems in your life. This is where chameleon medicine can help. Call on the chameleon to change things up, get wild, strike out boldly, and keep more than one perspective going at once.

Finally, chameleon medicine reminds us that we don't have to be center stage all the time. It can be exhausting to be on display, to be your best self all the time. Hiding gets a bad rap, but blending into the background a bit can give you a break and a little protection, which can allow for deeper contemplation and new insights. Plus, stepping back in this way might allow you to sneak up on your goals, in a stealthy new set of clothes . . .

Questions to Consider

- Have you recently felt hemmed in by the demands of life? Can you embrace your own wonderful weirdness in a way that gets you what you need on a deeper, more connected level?

- Is there a perspective you've held for a long time that might need to be updated? Can you expand your view?

- Have you been in the spotlight for a while? Do you have to be there now? What would happen if you stepped back to rest and recharge and plot your next bold move?

Calling the Spirit of the Chameleon

Chameleons and other reptiles are creatures of fire, which means they have a connection to the inner creativity and passion that burns in the center of our heart. Changing your colors is a powerful metaphor for creativity. If you are used to looking at a situation in one way, consider how it may look from a completely different perspective. If you are working on a difficult project that needs a fresh take, turn it upside down, even literally. You can't change your outlook without changing yourself. Are you willing to try that?

And if you need a break in order to refresh your creativity, take yourself out of the spotlight. Take a break from social media. Give yourself an at-home meditation and self-care retreat. Work from home and wear your sweatpants all day. Whether it's for quiet contemplation or just a chance to hide out and recharge—go for it. Add something chameleonlike to your personal altar or medicine bag to remind you that hiding can be an important adaptive response.

A Prayer for Chameleon Energy

Colorful cousin chameleon,
one of Mother Earth's most
creative creatures, help me to
find my true colors and to see
the world in a new light.

CHICKEN

Teachings to Remember When Encountering Chickens

Chickens call to mind the boisterous crowing of the rooster, which is so prevalent in popular media that we associate the sound with the start of a new day. Roosters crow multiple times during the day and for a variety of reasons, but this daybreak ruckus has become an iconic symbol for the dawn, a time to wake up, come alive, and begin the day's business with a fresh outlook. The animal wisdom in this case is more metaphorical than scientific, but just as meaningful for our personal journey.

Related animals: guinea hen, pheasant, quail, rooster, turkey

Elements: earth, air

- Optimistic
- Innovative
- Fertile

Once an uncommon sight in suburbs and cities, chickens have become extremely popular again. Keeping chickens in a backyard coop can provide practical and emotional gifts for years to come. Many people keep chickens so that they have fresh eggs, which, like the crow of a rooster, embodies newness.

Throughout human history, eggs have served as a powerful symbol for potential, wholeness, rebirth, new beginnings, and creation itself. Many creation myths tell of a great bird or a great egg from which the universe or the planet emerges. Eggs are part of worldwide celebrations of spring, a time of regeneration, fertility, and growth. Baby chicks remind us of the joy and fragility of new life.

Chickens spend much of their day scratching along the ground looking for insects. Reading this through the wisdom of the medicine wheel, we might say that chickens possess a practical, embodied intelligence, as a creature of air/mind who spends all its time digging in the earth. This may seem like a gentle, harmless scratch, but chickens tend to strip the grass from an entire area. Chickens remind us to put our mind to work in diligent pursuit of our goals and to fuel our passions by putting some persistent muscle behind our deepest desires.

Questions to Consider

- What is the next smallest physical action you can do to further one of your goals?

- Is now a time for newness in your life? What if you thought of some aspect of yourself as a tiny chick inside an egg, waiting to hatch? How would you nurture this little being and harness the power of rebirth and regeneration?

- What is calling you to wake up?

Calling the Spirit of the Chicken

This is an air cleansing ceremony taught to me by one of the most powerful healers I have ever known: my grandmother. She explained to me that in the cosmology of the body, the forehead is like a great sky, the place where eagles fly. This makes sense, as our mind is the seat of our imagination, and this space needs to be clear.

Gather an egg—whether it's from the grocery store or your backyard flock doesn't matter—and hold it gently. Close your eyes and take a few deep breaths to center yourself and commit to staying in the present moment. Then, slowly begin working the egg over your forehead and temples with the intent of clearing space. Whatever comes into your mind, just notice it and release it, as if you are letting go of a handful of leaves in the wind. Use your breath at the same time, focusing on healing, opening, and clearing space with each exhale. Finally, cup the egg in your hands and feel the air on your forehead as it caresses all the places the egg touched. Imagine the air absorbing and carrying away clouds or smoke in your mind's eye.

A Prayer for Chicken Energy

As rooster greets the dawn, by the teachings
of the mother hen and the chick newly hatched
from an egg round as the morning sun,
I welcome the new day, the new spring, the new rising
of great beginnings, into my life, my heart,
my spirit.

CICADA

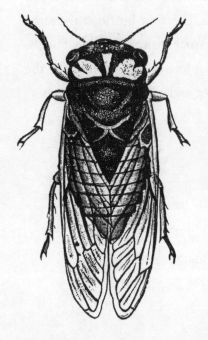

Teachings to Remember When Encountering Cicadas

Cicadas' song rings out for the length of summer, filling the humid nights with its steady hum. Some species have life cycles that keep them underground for an incredible sixteen to eighteen years, and others rise into their winged, cacophonous form once a year. Ancient literature from Greece to China speaks of this summer symphony, which cicadas make by vibrating two special music-producing organs called tymbals. They amplify the sound through their hollow abdomens, broadcasting their song through whole neighborhoods and across forests.

Related animals: cricket, katydid

Elements: air and earth

• Vocal
• Patient
• Transformative

The cicada has only a short window of time in which to attract the attention of a mate, so when the time comes they really need to be heard in order to continue their existence. Human beings also need to be heard. The cicada teaches us that we can develop our creativity at whatever pace works for us, and that when the time comes, it is our joy and our responsibility to amplify our intent and our uniqueness.

Some species of cicada spend almost their entire lives underground before emerging to sing their song, attract a mate, and die. Sometimes it takes a long time in the darkness, in the grounding presence of the rich, nourishing earth, in order to bring forward the work you were put here to do. There are countless stories of "late bloomer" artists, thinkers, scientists, and more—all of whom spent time fostering their talents in private before they found their voice in public.

If you grew up in a part of the country with annual cicadas, you might already be familiar with their molting habits. They leave their old exoskeletons behind as they transition into full adulthood. The fragile husks can be found all over tree trunks in summer, waiting to be marveled at and collected by fascinated children, and maybe a few adults looking for a power animal talisman. These ghostlike husks are potent symbols of regeneration and rebirth, reminding us that there is power in letting go of the old in order to transform and find our voice in a new way.

Questions to Consider

- Your voice represents your uniqueness, the gifts that you and only you can share with the world. Are you sharing your voice?

- What in your life could benefit from the spirit of regeneration? What can you release or shed to make room for new life?

- Is there something in your life that you are impatient to see come to fruition but that could benefit from further hibernation or development? Consider whether patience in this area might lead to a more satisfying outcome.

Calling the Spirit of the Cicada

Musicians and music lovers have a friend in the cicada. Their hypnotic, unending song can be as loud as a rock concert. Seek out the shells of molted cicadas on the trunks of trees and place them on your personal altar or another area that you pass by daily to remind you of their powerful energy of slow processes, rebirth, and regeneration.

If you feel drawn to the powerful spirit of the cicada, spend some time listening to their song and meditating on questions about how you might learn to amplify your voice in the world. Can you increase your network? Find more venues to share your work? What do you need to let go of in order to enter a new transformative chapter in your life?

A Prayer for Cicada Energy

Summer oaks hold
papery pieces of the past in their branches,
alive with the ceaseless song that says:
today, in this place, the cicada
fills its voice with everything it has.
Teach me, cicada, to do the same.

COW

See also: Bison, Goat, Sheep

Related animals: oxen, water buffalo, yak

Element: earth

• Nourishing
• Steady and calm
• Pensive

Teachings to Remember When Encountering Cows

We have lived alongside cows for millennia, and they hold a special place in the sacred scriptures of many world religions. Hindus consider cows to be sacred animals, and in certain parts of India their slaughter is banned. In ancient Egypt, the cow was associated with fertility. Several Egyptian goddesses were linked with cow imagery, including Hathor, a goddess of joy, love, and beauty.

We tend to take cows for granted, sometimes even considering them silly or cartoonish creatures. We can honor the gravity and calmness of these beings, as well as their warmth and connectedness to each other and their human stewards, when they are raised in a caring and conscientious way. Nuzzling to the earth, making their way slowly and steadily, cows relate to being grounded and present.

Nourishment is a major theme in the element of earth. The mother cow gives nutrient-rich milk to her calves, and to humans who consume dairy as well. Milk is a symbol of new life and nourishment in many cultures.

Part of the cow's digestive process famously includes a stage called cud chewing, in which the cow reserves food in one of its several stomachs until it can properly chew it, in which case it regurgitates the food back into its mouth. This is a great teaching, especially for our fast-paced, short-attention-span times. Life may move fast, and information even faster. We can gain new wisdom and insight by setting some things aside and returning to them later with a little more space and perspective. Take a "cow moment" to stop, think, and digest the events of your day. This kind of mindful consideration helps us process our lives at a healthy pace.

Questions to Consider

- In what ways are you nourished in spirit? How can you contribute physical, emotional, or spiritual nourishment to your community?

- Are there any areas of life that would benefit from some weighty consideration, perhaps by mulling over different options with others?

- Do you practice a form of mindfulness? How can you cultivate more peace and gentle gravity in your life?

Calling the Spirit of the Cow

Chances are good that you can find some cows nearby or outside of your city where you might be able to observe them at their steady best. Consider visiting a local dairy that employs permaculture practices, in which farming and raising animals can help repair Mother Earth in a nourishing cycle.

One practice that might help you slow down and mindfully "chew" over your day is the meditative exercise of thinking through the day backward. At the end of the day, find a comfortable spot and allow your mind to replay the events in reverse. See how many details you can remember as you do so; if there are any places that you feel stuck on, make a note to contemplate those in more depth later, perhaps through journaling or healing meditation. When we slow down like this, we notice more, and this kind of awareness seeds the pasture for true inner peace.

A Prayer for Cow Energy

Guiding light, gentle presence,
mother cow, let me be nourished
by the simple, earthy space of pure being.
Help me rest in the deep peace of contemplation.

COYOTE

Teachings to Remember When Encountering Coyotes
With its long legs, ears pricked up, and bushy tail lowered, the coyote skulks through plains, farms, and urban neighborhoods in an ever-widening territorial range. In the Americas, the coyote has long been one of the most sacred power animals, its name an altered form of the Nahuatl word *coyotl*. The coyote is by turns an old rogue, a goofy trickster, and a noble warrior. The mythological coyote plays a central role in many Native creation stories, bringing the power of fire to the people as well as freeing the buffalo to roam the plains, among other feats.

See also: Crow, Fox, Rabbit, Spider, Wolf

Related animals: hyena, jackal

Element: earth

- Stealthy and cunning
- Changeable
- Paradoxical

In the wild, coyotes are cunning and have been known to employ all kinds of "tricks" both in the hunt and as defensive maneuvers. Stalking in a pack, one animal will playfully lure away a dog who is protecting a chicken coop or flock of sheep so that the other coyotes can move in unchallenged. Coyotes will fake an injury to lure a predator away from the vulnerable pups in their den, and they'll even play dead to attract their victims, snatching a meal when someone comes to investigate.

The coyote is a trickster like the crow, spider, and rabbit, but its slippery, changeable nature is unique. It's easy to see how myths and legends paint him as a hero and friend to people one moment, as a greedy, egotistic antihero the next, and as a wise fool always getting into (and out of) trouble after that. In fact, this is an essential facet of coyote medicine—being hard to pin down, shapeshifting, having the ability and willingness to change, and embracing paradox.

The psychologist Carl Jung wrote that "the paradox is one of our most valued spiritual possessions," claiming that "only the paradox comes anywhere near to comprehending the fullness of life." This is perhaps the greatest lesson of the coyote, and the most difficult one to grasp. By its nature, a paradox straddles two or more opposing things in a kind of dynamic tension. We can almost *feel* a paradox in our body. It doesn't make sense and we can't understand it rationally. Paradox makes us uncomfortable even as it energizes our knowing in a new way. Paradox reflects truth itself.

Coyotes embody contradiction. For the precolonial people of the Americas, the coyote was a symbol of warrior might. The story of the coyote today in some ways reflects a conqueror's story—settlers decided that the strength of a "defeated" people should be thought of thereafter as deception, greed, and cowardice. Today, coyotes are sometimes hated and feared for their predation of pets and livestock. Yet many people love them, and admire the beauty of a wild animal so willing and able to thrive in our midst. Wary and curious, stealthy and unseen one moment and then obnoxiously loud, with their yipping group howls in the middle of the night. Scary and harmless, nurturing and careless—the coyote wields the power of truth in the form of paradox.

Questions to Consider

- Have you struggled with contradicting traits or impulses within yourself? Can you see the strengths in your flaws and the flaws in your strengths?

- Would you rather be right or would you rather seek the truth?

- Are there stories in your life that have completely changed over time?

Calling the Spirit of the Coyote

Warning: the coyote may surprise and even frustrate you when you ask him for help or support. However, if you can stay open and keep a sense of humor about this peculiar, shapeshifting medicine, it can be especially potent.

Paradoxes permeate literature, all the sciences, mythology, philosophy, mathematics, and spirituality. The fact that we think of them as anomalies when they are so universal is in itself a kind of paradox. One profound way to call the spirit of coyote to your side is to carry a paradox in your pocket. It could be a symbol such as a Celtic knot, an image or drawing like those of M. C. Escher, or the text of a riddle or puzzle. It could be a Zen koan—a riddle with no answer, such as, "What is the sound of one hand clapping?" In the morning, take a few moments to sit quietly with your paradox. Then slip it into your pocket and forget about it. If you are looking for help with a particular problem, invite the spirit of the coyote to play with this riddle throughout the day on the edges of your consciousness. As you are getting undressed at the end of the day, remove the paradox from your pocket and look at it again, taking in any new meaning or perspective it holds for you. If you want, you can place it on your altar or in your medicine bag as a reminder of coyote's awesome and maddening power.

A Prayer for Coyote Energy

Brother coyote, warrior, fool, and sage,
invite me into your world and
help me see the paradox in all things.
With a sly grin and swish of your tail
guide me to knowing the unknowable truth.

CRANE

Teachings to Remember When Encountering Cranes

Considered holy in many Eastern traditions, and widely revered and celebrated in folklore of cultures all around the world, the graceful crane makes its home in water, earth, and sky. Seeing a crane makes us gasp in reverence for the natural world. We delight in the grace and beauty of a creature whose shapes and proportions are so different from our own, a leggy, agile example of the astonishing diversity of our home, Mother Earth. In artwork and stories, cranes are linked to luck, prosperity, and immortality, as well as vigilance and wariness. For many of us, their cultural significance overshadows our tangible experience observing cranes—a fact that only adds to their mysterious attraction.

See also: Swan

Related animals: bittern, egret, heron

Elements: air, water, earth

- Joyful
- Eternal
- Vigilant

One folktale about the crane tells us that when a group of them sleeps, one crane keeps watch through the night, holding a stone in one foot so that if it falls asleep, the stone drops and alerts the crane to stay vigilant. This story builds the observation that waterbirds sometimes stand or sleep on one foot, but it also points in a more poetic way to the crane being a protector of community and family, especially through the power of its vigilance. If you've ever seen a slow-moving crane stalking its prey in the water, you have seen this hyperalertness at work.

Many cranes also perform elaborate mating dances, so we associate them with joy and celebration, as well as romance and long relationships. Humans tap into crane energy in their own dancing, some directly derived from the crane's movement. The joy and celebration of dance brings harmony to the body and mind and can also help build profound connection with other people. It's almost impossible to be in a bad mood while dancing.

Questions to Consider

- Can you take a moment for a dance break today? Better yet, can you pull your partner, family, or other loved ones into your dance?

- What do you say or think when you see a crane? Next time you see one, perhaps it can be a reminder to cultivate grace, joy, or vigilance in your life.

- How easy or difficult are transitions in your life? In what way can you bring a little bit of support and grace to yourself as you move through change?

Calling the Spirit of the Crane

We can call upon the crane to help us move with ease through transitions and phases. Think of the elements of the medicine wheel and how the crane travels effortlessly between the quadrants of air (the mind), earth (the body), and water (emotions). Moving between the different aspects of ourselves in a graceful way too, from student to teacher to elder, can bring a sense of purpose and longevity to any intention.

When you know you are being asked to work within multiple elements, facets of your personality, or divergent tasks, try a crane meditation. Close your eyes and take a few deep, centering breaths. When you're ready, focus on the places where you can feel the pull of the earth's gravity—your feet or the parts of you that are resting on a chair. Then imagine you are slowly being filled up with water, from your toes to the top of your head. Feel the flow. Extend your awareness out into the air and the space around you. Let it lift up and lighten your physical body. You can then cycle between each of these sensations in your mind's eye, imagining the ease of the crane as you do and remembering that you are at home and welcomed in all of them.

How do you celebrate important moments in your life? Do you gather your friends and family together? Do you mark the occasion with a special ritual? Experiencing the joy of success, or even just of everyday life, invokes the spirit of the crane.

Have you done any dancing lately? If it's been a while, consider putting this book down right this minute, playing some music you love, and dancing wherever you are for just a few minutes. If you're in public and can inspire someone else to laugh and dance too, all the better! There is always something to celebrate and there is always time to dance.

A Prayer for Crane Energy

Graceful, dancing crane sisters,
watchful and grounded in the joy
of everyday beauty, teach me how
to find peace in every moment. Help me
to dance through my days in celebration
of being and to transition with poise.

CROW

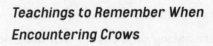

Teachings to Remember When Encountering Crows

Perched on a branch or a wire, the silhouette of the crow cuts a sleek black figure against the sky. With their piercing, knowing eyes, distinctive calls, acrobatic flying, and gurgling vocalizations, a visit from these highly intelligent birds feels like a special occasion. Renowned for their problem-solving and curiosity, with a touch of mischievous cleverness, crows connote insight, memory, and the power of the unknown. They are sometimes associated with darkness, death, or war, particularly as messengers, such as in Edgar Allan Poe's famous poem *The Raven*. Yet as is the case in so much of animal medicine, the opposite holds true as well. Crow medicine can bring healing, magical energy into our lives.

See also: Coyote, Fox, Rabbit, Spider

Related animals: blackbird, grackle, jackdaw, magpie, parrot, raven

Elements: air

• Clever and curious
• Intelligent
• Healing

As creatures of air on the medicine wheel, birds are associated with the mind. Crows and ravens belong to the exceptionally intelligent *Corvidae* family and are among the very few animals who will fashion sticks and other implements into tools to gather food or make toys to play with. The Norse god Odin had two raven companions named Thought and Memory who whispered important information into his ears. And in several American Indian cultures of the Pacific Northwest, the raven is a clever trickster figure and the creator of the earth. In some stories, the raven is responsible for fixing the sun, moon, and stars in the sky, and for stealing fire from the heavens to help people on earth find a way to warm themselves in winter and cook their food.

Crows are known to have excellent memories, recognize other individuals in their communities, use tools, and work together to find and procure food. Spending time observing crows can be very rewarding—they are quick, lively birds, and you can often see them as they work to find solutions to whatever obstacle is in their way. They also sometimes seem to be observing us in turn, curious about who is watching them, and even wild ravens are known to bring "gifts" like shiny paper clips or bits of string to humans with whom they have a relationship. Like other animals who use tools, they seem to have a consciousness of self that is fascinating, and yet they are so different in shape and physicality from us. Ravens and crows show us that when we use our creative problem-solving skills, we can achieve things we may have thought were impossible.

While there are plenty of references to ravens and crows as symbols of darkness, observing them in nature reveals their true nature. Lighthearted and dynamic, they approach problems with diligence and creative thinking, using unexpected resources and relying on others in their community. Corvids embody thinking outside the box and may even bring insights and healing from an unseen realm.

Questions to Consider

- What serious problem in your life might benefit from a more light-hearted and curious approach?

- Have you ever had a special encounter with a crow or raven? Thinking back, were there any special insights or new ways of thinking that came from that time?

Calling the Spirit of the Crow

Corvids are able to remember an astonishing number of things, including human and animal faces, other birds in their community, where stashes of food are hidden, and much more. To invoke the spirit of this intelligent, light-hearted trickster ally, spend some time exercising your brain with memory games or puzzles.

The next time you feel bogged down by a problem, consider the problem-solving nature of the raven, the jackdaw, the rook, and the crow. One of the great teachings of a trickster is the importance of not taking yourself too seriously. Tricksters often mess up, but they invariably dust themselves off and keep going. Try thinking about your problem in a different way. Turn the problem upside down or break it into pieces. How would you solve it if you had different tools at your disposal?

A Prayer for Crow Energy

Brother raven, sister crow, bright and smart,
thought, memory, and laugher. Help me
think about this differently—help me
see what I am missing, how I can use
my mind to solve what my hands cannot.

DEER

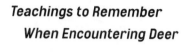

Teachings to Remember
When Encountering Deer

There is something magical about deer. Their sleek grace has inspired humankind through the ages, and a majestic stag with full antlers has long been a symbol of nobility and strength. Deer have a lightness when they move through the forest or open fields that evokes beauty, dance, and freedom.

Coming upon a group of deer in the woods feels like stumbling into a time out of time, with perhaps only the sound of the wind in the trees and the hushed crackling of leaves underfoot. We enter into the presence of deer by bringing our energy in tune with theirs. This is a sacred moment, made precious by the fact that this natural silence could be so easily broken, the deer so easily

See also: Horse

Related animals: antelope, elk, moose, reindeer

Element: earth

- Swift and graceful
- Transformative
- Aware

startled. We become deerlike—immersing ourselves without thinking in silent awareness of our own body and everything our senses can perceive in the world around us. In this way, encounters with deer are moments of pure mindfulness.

They make no noise and only look at us, ears twitching, all their senses attuned to the moment. Then, perhaps in response to some inner knowing, or the lightest sound of a breaking twig, they startle away, fast and fleet.

Nearly all male deer have antlers, and in some species of deer females occasionally will have them as well. In yearly cycles, deer will shed an entire set of antlers in order to develop a larger set. We too require this kind of clearing out to make way for the new, and deer medicine can remind us that we can let go of the old in order to foster new growth or accept new gifts.

Questions to Consider

- How might you tap into timeless awareness? What grace-filled silence can you cultivate in your life?

- When was the last time you reorganized your living space and let go of the old in order to make way for new energy?

- Can you move through your day with the attentive presence of the deer? What does it mean to travel lightly and swiftly on an energetic level?

Calling the Spirit of the Deer

Deer populations are so large in some areas that they annoy people by munching on gardens and destroying young trees. Deer are also attuned to danger and tend to drop some of their protective instincts when there are few predators, which can make them easier to spend time with. Nonetheless, to be in their presence, you will have to walk out into the world, and probably into the woods, keeping your steps careful and silent, and your mind watchful. Be a contemplative hunter—you aren't looking for game to feed your family, you are hunting beauty, silence, and grace. You are hunting magic, in search of a timeless moment in which your awareness expands and you hold the whole forest in your heart.

A Prayer for Deer Energy

May I be as light, as fleet,
as swift as the wind, as full of joy,
as unmatched in grace,
as the silent doe, as noble
as the antlered stag behind the trees,
who waits and watches me bow my head
as I pass by.

DOG

See also: Wolf, Fox, Coyote

Related animals: dingo, hyena, wild dog

Element: earth

- Loyal, loving, and devoted
- Helpful and enthusiastic
- Emotional

Teachings to Remember When Encountering Dogs

The dog has been our constant companion for eons. We have long relied on their strength, keen senses, wits, and loyalty for everything from companionship to protection, from farming to herding to guiding. The bond between dogs and humans is said to be at least fifteen thousand years old, and maybe even older. The domestic dogs and cats we live with today are also thought to have descended from wild creatures who made the choice to hang around our human ancestors. That is, the relationship has long been mutually beneficial and respectful.

Whether they are trained or bred for a specific task or not, dogs tend to be eager and helpful, excited to learn and motivated by play and reward. Some dogs even suffer or become destructive when they don't have a job. Sometimes we forget this powerful medicine of the dog, which is about just showing up in the present moment, excited about life and ready to help.

I admit, I am biased. I have four little dogs at home, and no matter what kind of day I may be having, when I walk in the front door they are always happy to see me. They are thrilled when it's time to eat a meal or go outside. They go wild with excitement when anyone comes to the door. They curl up into a ball and fall into a deep, satisfying sleep whenever they get the chance. They remind me to enjoy the simple, bodily pleasures as creatures of the earth. Most of all, I'm grateful that I get to share my life with these dogs, who let me know they love me no matter what. Their genuine affection and loyal devotion lift my spirits every day.

The dog's gift for showing love and affection is a great teaching that helps to counterbalance what can feel like relentless bad news and negativity—in our media and online especially. What if we emulated our friend the dog and radiated pure love out into the world each day? What if we greeted each day, each person, and each new adventure the way a dog greets its favorite person coming home? That kind of enthusiasm and genuine love lifts us all up.

Questions to Consider

- How do you let your love shine through in joyful and even silly or over-the-top ways? Can you find the means to help lift the spirits of someone you care about today by spreading that joyful enthusiasm?

- What are you loyal to? Is it true for you or something you feel tied to out of domestication or habit? Can you bring your loyalties into even truer expressions of your inner intent?

- Can you offer help where it is least expected today, without looking for anything in return?

Calling the Spirit of the Dog

If you live with a dog, you have a great teacher with you all the time. If not, there are so many different dogs to observe out in the world and countless enchanting videos. Animal shelters and rescues are often looking for helping hands as well, which is another way to interact with dogs.

The next time you feel isolated and alone, or if you've had a hard day, call on the spirit of this loving animal. Do a little dance of excitement before a walk or a delicious meal. Spread the love by taking a few minutes to call a friend or visit a family member. See if you can share a smile or a good laugh with them. Not only will you brighten their day, but I guarantee that you will feel better yourself. This is the powerful reciprocity that lives in dog medicine: when you give love and attention to others, you will receive it in return.

Finally, you might try connecting with dog energy through a lovingkindness meditation. After settling in and taking a few deep breaths, call to mind a person or a beloved animal for whom it's very easy to feel warmth and affection. Feel any sensations that come up with this—blood flowing to your face and chest, tingling or warmth, a smile or laughter. This lovingkindness is available to you at any time.

A Prayer for Dog Energy

Loving dog, kind and playful, loyal and faithful,
teach me how to love the world with abandon.
Help me show those I love how much I care about them,
and show me how to be a helper and friend to all I meet.

DOLPHIN

See also: Otter, Seal, Whale

Related animals: manatee, sea lion

Element: water

- Joyful
- Free
- Communicative and community-oriented

Teachings to Remember When Encountering Dolphins

Anytime I go to the ocean I scan the water for dolphins, and when I see a fin rising and dipping in the waves, I get an electric jolt of bliss. Dolphins have been a symbol of luck and joy for ages and appear in ancient art and mythology all over the world. In addition to being playful, curious, and friendly, dolphins are known to help others in their immediate community, as well as other animals who are sick, injured, or in danger—including humans.

Dolphins seem to take unbridled delight in racing up near boats, leaping through the air, and playing games with each other. Just watching them can lift the darkest mood. Their zest for life is bold and contagious, and to human eyes they seem to be always smiling and laughing. Indeed, dolphins are gregarious and community-oriented, forging strong bonds from birth and living in sophisticated social groups throughout their lives. These groups are strengthened by the dolphin's ability to communicate with a wide array of vocalizations. They even have distinct names for themselves and one another.

The dolphin is of course a creature of the water quadrant of the medicine wheel, the realm of summer, adolescence, and emotion. From early on, many of us take in strict domestication relating to emotion, often along the lines of "control yourself," "calm down," or "you're too much." In adolescence, we experience an emotional roller coaster of overwhelming emotions related to hormones and brain growth, and it can cause a lot of suffering when these feelings run headlong into the messages from society that tell us how we should or should not feel and behave.

Dolphin medicine reminds us that we can relish the full expression of our authentic emotion, all the while knowing that feelings are always flowing like water, and today's feelings will be tomorrow's memories or lessons if we let them pass through us freely. Laugh loudly, says the dolphin. Weep in a place you feel safe. Your animal body is simply experiencing an emotion. I like to think that, given the opportunity, the dolphin would reject the pretense of social media, where we tend to hide our worst moments and only show the best aspects of our lives.

Dolphins relish the flow of life and don't hide their grief or their joy. They cultivate a rich inner freedom, leaping and playing, protecting and connecting with those they care about. When we let emotions flow, we can also let them go when they are no longer needed. Repressing our feelings only allows them to fester and linger in unhealthy ways. Learning how to understand, express, and eventually let go of our real feelings instead of hiding them is one of the critical first steps toward inner freedom.

Questions to Consider

- What is calling you toward joy right now? How can you express that joy to others?

- Is there an area of your life that could benefit from improved communication?

- What emotions tend to get bottled up? Do you push down your rage and frustration? Do you mute your enjoyment and passion? What about sadness? What would happen if you let it all flow?

Calling the Spirit of the Dolphin

To bring the dolphin's playful spirit into your life, you may want to do some journaling about how you've processed your emotions up to this point. Dig into your particular domestications—the messages and lessons you learned when you were younger about emotions (often from well-meaning relatives and teachers). Think about the extent to which these domestications hold true for you today and how they may hold you back from letting emotions flow naturally through you. Call on the wisdom of the dolphin to support you before, during, and after such intense journaling and personal inventory.

A Prayer for Dolphin Energy

Leaping dolphin, friend and ally in joy,
help me open my heart to the kind of
inner freedom you embody. Make my heart
free as an arrow darting through
clear emotional waters.

DOVE

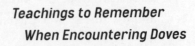

Teachings to Remember When Encountering Doves

For thousands of years, the dove has symbolized beauty, peace, grace, and communication. In ancient Mesopotamia and Greece, doves were associated with goddesses of love and beauty such as Inanna-Ishtar and Aphrodite. Doves bring peace and good news, as in the Hebrew scriptures when Noah releases a dove to see if the flood has ended and the bird returns with an olive branch in its mouth. Hebrew and Christian scriptures evoke the spirit of God or the Holy Spirit in the dove, and we see its image everywhere in religious, secular, and political artwork.

The dove belongs to the north quadrant of the medicine wheel, the element of air, and occupies the place of a teacher of teachers. Many of the most powerful human teachers in the world share qualities with the dove: they seem to see clearly and have the ability to spread messages of peace and divine love far and wide. We do not have to be a master of peace to align ourselves with dove medicine. We can remember, for example, that doves (like their relatives the homing pigeons)

See also: Swan, Penguin

Related animals: lovebird, mourning dove, pigeon

Element: air

- Peaceful
- Optimistic
- Gentle

are messengers and harbingers, usually of good news. Keeping the lines of communication open can help resolve conflict and bring peace. It can also simply bring us into closer communication with the natural world. I have a friend, for example, who lives in Texas, and through observation she noticed that when she heard the unique call of mourning doves outside, usually in February, this was a sign that spring was around the corner.

Dove medicine raises our levels of positivity and joy, delivers good news and hope in times of struggle, and bridges the gulf between opposing sides. The next time you are in a difficult situation, consider how the teaching of the dove may influence how you communicate with others. Are you a voice for peace and resolution? Do you bring the hope and clarity of the dove?

Questions to Consider

- How can you contribute to peace in your life, the lives of those around you, and the greater world? Are there personal or inner conflicts you can tend to that would bring added peace into your life?

- What does the concept of lovingkindness look like in your everyday routine? How can you increase lovingkindness toward others, even those with whom you struggle?

- Sometimes good news might seem hard to find—do you take time to seek out good news and share it with your community?

Calling the Spirit of the Dove

There are species of dove in nearly every geographical region on earth, so finding doves in your area shouldn't be difficult. And while many people think of pigeons as pests, it's important to remember that pigeons and doves are in the same family and have the same gifts! The papery song created by a flock of startled pigeons or doves lifting off from the ground can be found in city squares as easily as wooded areas. Their cooing and fluffing can calm and soothe our inner turmoil.

To connect with the spirit of the dove, consider actions and meditations that invite feelings of inner peace, love, and goodwill into your spiritual routine, such as the Buddhist tradition of *metta*, or lovingkindness meditation. A simple exercise is to close your eyes, take a few deep, slow breaths, and imagine a dove in the center of your chest. As you breathe in, the dove opens its beautiful white wings, and as you exhale, it settles them down into a silent, peaceful stillness. Continue this until you feel the innate peace of the dove begin to infuse every part of your heart and mind.

A Prayer for Dove Energy

Winged messenger, graceful dove,
bearer of the olive branch,
lend me your gentleness.
Help me to find the path to peaceful communication
in every part of my life.

DRAGONFLY

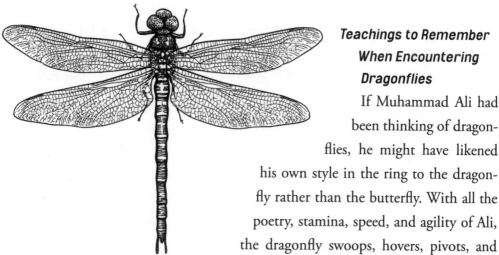

Teachings to Remember When Encountering Dragonflies

If Muhammad Ali had been thinking of dragon-flies, he might have likened his own style in the ring to the dragon-fly rather than the butterfly. With all the poetry, stamina, speed, and agility of Ali, the dragonfly swoops, hovers, pivots, and dives. Male dragonflies will fight for territory and mates. They can see 360 degrees. Each of their four wings moves independently, allowing them to fly in any direction, including backward, and they are strong enough to fly across oceans. Beings of the air, dragonflies spend their lives in or near water, mak-ing them a great power animal to approach when issues of mental clarity and emotion intersect. These creatures also predate the dinosaurs, and some of their ancestors took to the skies with a wingspan of over two feet. The structure of their body is much the same today as it was then, and part of their medicine is this evolutionary steadiness. Humans came on the scene so recently, and we have a lot to learn from those creatures that have been thriving just as they are for millennia.

See also: Butterfly, Hummingbird

Related animals: damselfly

Elements: air and water

- Agile, enduring, and flexible
- Thriving
- Happy

Like butterflies and hummingbirds, dragonflies are known for their bright iridescent colors, their wings catching the light of the day. They can look a bit like flying jewels, belying their power as fully evolved, highly attuned animals whose every feature and attribute serve their intention to eat, mate, and prosper. The dragonfly reminds us that we can access this kind of alignment in body and intent as well, when we uncover the truth about ourselves and remember that we already have everything we need.

Many cultures consider the dragonfly a positive symbol, and in Japan the dragonfly is a symbol of happiness. They embody a certain lightness, both as colorful suncatchers and in the way they hover and float. It's no coincidence that we link happiness metaphorically with lightness. We say things like "my heart became light," or we're "walking on air" or have "a spring in our step." When we connect to our heart's true happiness, we often feel physically lighter.

Questions to Consider

- Have you felt lighthearted lately? If not, can you think of a way to set down your burdens a bit, even just for a moment?

- Have you been asked by a friend or colleague to look at a situation in a different way and you've been resistant? Now may be a good time to reevaluate whether your attachment to being right has prevented you from being flexible and light.

- Do you think you are enough just as you are? Learning and improving throughout our lifetime is a worthy goal, and yet the truth is that we are already whole and can thrive just as we are.

Calling the Spirit of the Dragonfly

Happiness can sometimes feel elusive, and when we don't have regular touchstones of joy, life can quickly become dark and heavy. Sometimes we think of happiness as an all-or-nothing proposition and get caught up in our own stories about future happiness or happy memories of the past. In truth, happiness can only be found in one place: the present moment. We can locate and nurture it in tiny increments, in a focused and mindful way.

One practice to cultivate more happiness is keeping a gratitude journal, which creates a simple yet powerful feedback loop. By finding even the smallest thing that made you happy and being grateful for it, you generate even more happiness, which in turn makes you even more grateful. Make a practice of writing down three things per day that you are grateful for. This can be something as small as finding a new bean sprout in your garden or as life-changing as being offered an amazing new job. There's no need to write elaborate entries for this if you don't want to—just jot down one sentence or even one word for each thing you're grateful for. Take a moment to really breathe in the feeling that each thing generates, allowing it to bring a smile to your face or a flush of warmth to your chest. You can do this in a few minutes each day or incorporate it into a deeper ritual practice at your altar or in another meaningful place.

A Prayer for Dragonfly Energy

Dragonfly, bright as sunlight,
floating and flashing on the clear waters
in my heart; help me find one moment
every day to embrace the sweet happiness
of a life spent exploring this living world.

EAGLE

Teachings to Remember When Encountering Eagles

In the natural world and in our human stories, the eagle holds enormous power. As some of the largest birds in the world with incredibly strong beaks, talons, and wings, they have a commanding presence and a piercing, serious gaze that surveys all it sees. Eagle has long been the personal power animal of nobility in a variety of cultures and is often displayed as a symbol of military strength and pride. For times in your life when you may need to draw on all your reserves and stand proudly by your convictions, the eagle is a powerful ally to call upon.

See also: Hawk, Vulture

Related animals: condor, falcon

Element: air

• Powerful and strong
• Brave
• Authoritative and decisive

The eagle rules the sky and is the most formidable power animal when it comes to the realm of the mind. The mind is our only tool for creating the powerful Personal Dream of our own lives, as well as contributing to the collective Dream of the Planet. We underestimate this power in ourselves quite often, believing that we are ruled by forces outside of our control. Eagle reminds us that this is not true. Our mind is a powerful tool that will keep churning out powerful stories whether we are conscious of this process or not. When we learn to wield this tool for our own best interest and in expression of our truest intent, the mind becomes as commanding as the eagle itself, with unparalleled clarity of vision and strength of purpose.

The eagle has no time or patience for negative self-talk and destructive fantasies. Real power, strength, and authority come from organic confidence rooted in a deep connection to truth instead of illusion. As a being of pure clarity, the eagle radiates confidence and teaches those who are willing to learn how to cultivate it in their own lives.

This clarity of vision affords the eagle its commanding presence and natural authority. We sometimes think that authority is something bestowed on us by outside forces, as in degrees, ranks, or titles. But the truth is that the ability to speak with real authority comes from clarity. Experience and knowledge can also grant a certain amount of authority, but a child can express a deep truth with utter conviction in her heart. In that moment, the child is a powerful authority because of her simple clarity and confidence. When clarity becomes the focus, the person who speaks with real authority is never afraid to admit when they don't know something or when they have been wrong. Why? Because they know that it's more important to preserve and protect the truth than to maintain an image.

It takes courage to summon one's own power and assert true confidence and authority. The eagle does not promise ease or comfort, but rather teaches the true meaning of power.

Questions to Consider

- What are the qualities of leadership you most admire? How can you cultivate those qualities in yourself?

- Are you in a situation that calls for personal courage? Are there others you can reach out to who might inspire you to take heart and face your fear with grace?

• Do you feel comfortable telling the truth? What about taking decisive action?

Calling the Spirit of the Eagle

Courage comes from the French root word *cor*, which means "heart." Courage comes from within, when one's heart is full and the mind is clear. To cultivate courage, authority, and power, one practice that will call on the powerful eagle as your guide is to do the hard work of facing your personal fears. When it comes to fears, the best way to do battle is not to fight at all, but rather to understand them in all their complexity. This is the kind of clarity that builds courage. Train your own eagle eye to understand yourself and your fears and they will no longer keep you from your heart's desire.

This kind of work may be done with a combination of journaling, ceremony, meditation, and self-reflection, and it may even be helpful to pursue counseling to help you work through more complicated knots.

A Prayer for Eagle Energy

Mentor eagle, powerful guide,
surveying the world from the clear skies
with a keen eye, an open heart, and
the authority that comes from clarity,
teach me to listen to my inner truth,
to have the confidence and knowledge
to meet every challenge
with the strength of mountains.

EARTHWORM

Earthworms are the epitome of being literally grounded. They spend their entire lives in the soil. What's more, every movement they make and every thing they eat and digest actually *makes* soil. In this way you could say that earthworms are made of the earth, and the ground we walk on is made by earthworms. Worms are great recyclers. As if by magic, they turn waste and dead matter into new life. We used to think of the food chain, with apex predators at the top and worms and other invertebrates at the very bottom. The food web feels like a more apt metaphor and restores the lowly worm to its rightful place, restoring energy to Mother Earth as all creatures grow and die.

Related animals: glowworm, inchworm, jumping worm, silkworm

Element: earth

- Humble
- Hands-on
- In it for the long haul

As part of that same old hierarchical story of the food chain, we think of worms as "lowly." And a synonym of lowly, "humble." The word *humble* actually has the same root as the word *humus*, meaning "soil." To be humble therefore is to be grounded, to be close to the earth. Humility is a virtue that we have somewhat dismissed in modern times, with some good reason. In many ways, the Western notion of humility, derived from religious traditions that elevate hierarchy, has left a legacy of self-debasement in its wake that doesn't have to be true for us anymore. Leaders and clergy long separated and celebrated the spiritual over the material in Western culture, justifying the subjugation of women, people of color, and animals. This also cut people off from their sacred relationships with the natural world.

Humility in this context has been distorted to mean having no self-worth, or beating yourself up emotionally. But true, healthy humility can be beneficial, restful, and positive. To be humble, as we learn from the simple earthworm, is to be close to Mother Earth, to be grounded and open, without the loud, clanging clutter of our own thoughts. To be humble is to be a good listener, to choose to serve justice out of a place of love, to relish silence, and to take time to consider the impact of your words before you speak. Real, healthy humility is not about denigrating yourself or being unworthy, it is about stepping out of your own way so that inspiration, spirit, and life can flow easily through you, and you can flow through life, just as the earthworm both glides through the soil and allows the soil to move through it.

Healthy, nourishing soil is the bedrock of life. Without it, plants can't thrive. Without plants, nothing else can survive. This is a great metaphor for the self. We all need to be nourished at a deep, spiritual level in order to thrive, but what nourishes you may be different than what nourishes your neighbor.

Questions to Consider

- What nourishes you? What can you do to build "better soil" in your life? What can you add or subtract to your daily routine that will help build a life full of rich, nourishing wisdom?

- What would healthy humility look like for you? Have you been the center of attention a lot lately? Can you take a break and spend some time being grounded, unseen, silent?

- Have you felt unmoored lately? Pulled into flights of fancy and fruitless mental gymnastics? This may be a perfect time to get grounded.

Calling the Spirit of the Earthworm

A great way to connect to the spirit of the earthworm is to get your hands in some actual dirt. There have been studies that show that working closely with natural, organic, healthy soil can actually lift your mood. Even if you have no place for a garden, you can start with a pot of earth in which you plant a single seed. You might even incorporate some ritual into it. Before you plant, hold the seed in your hands and close your eyes. Take three deep breaths that help ground you in the present moment, and imagine that the seed represents something you'd like to bring in closer in your life; this might be love, abundance, creativity, or anything that's meaningful to you. As you imagine the seed growing tall and strong, think about the power it represents overflowing in your life. As you plant and water the seed, thank it for its work in the world, and refresh your intention on occasion by meditating with your growing plant on the intention you originally imbued it with. Invoke the humble power of the earthworm to help in this process.

A Prayer for Earthworm Energy

Humble earthworm, who carries Mother Earth
in and through your life, help me to find a healthy
humility that will open my heart to helping others;
show me how to embrace the wisdom of the
small and lowly. Teach me the power that lies
hidden within the rich, dark earth, in even the
tiniest seed.

ELEPHANT

Teachings to Remember When Encountering Elephants

Gentle giant, strong protector, wise elder—the elephant has captured our imagination and inspired reverence for thousands of years. Their easygoing manner and steady, grounded way of moving through the world have become emblematic of the virtues of dignity, gravitas, and inner strength. They embody a gratifying paradox: even at their enormous size and with the thickness of their skin, their bodies are remarkably sensitive to touch, pressure, and even vibration. They can "hear" the vibrations of other elephants and goings on miles away through the soles of their feet. Their prehensile trunks are a sensory gold mine of smell and touch. In some religious traditions in Asia, the elephant is revered as a god, as in the case of the popular Indian deity Ganesha, who has the body of a man and the head of an elephant. Ganesha's attributes include wisdom, removing obstacles, and new beginnings.

Elephants form lasting social bonds and care for the others in their family group. Like humans, dolphins, chimps, and a few other animals, elephants

See also: Whale

Related animals: manatee, rhinoceros, woolly mammoth

Element: earth

- Kind and empathetic
- Family-oriented
- Dignified and rarefied

appear to help their sick friends and family members and grieve over their beloved dead. While they can be aggressive at certain life stages or when protecting themselves or their young, elephants are more often playful and inquisitive. The matriarchal leader of a group of elephants, often a grandmother, is the keeper of a vast store of memories and knowledge. She remembers the locations of food and water in different seasons, and she seems to confer with her counterparts on important decisions.

The world can only benefit from more kindness and empathy, and the elephant reminds us that as we move through each day, we can always share moments of goodness and support with others. Sometimes even a simple hug or pat on the shoulder can mean so much to someone who is suffering. The spiritual lesson of elephant medicine is the cultivation of empathy. Empathy happens when we listen deeply and make space for the truth of another person, when we locate a memory in ourselves that stirs connection, and when we feel with someone else in our physical body. When was the last time you listened to a friend without following their story with one of your own? We all fall into this habit sometimes, but the next time you are listening to someone share a difficult time with you, consider the wisdom of the elephant, and let them know that you hear them and support them, with no expectation of anything in return. Ask them gentle questions or simply sit with them in communal presence, with all the strength and gentleness of the elephant.

Questions to Consider

- How can you add a little more kindness to your life, your world, or your day? Are you being given an opportunity to listen deeply to someone else?

- Are there any obstacles in your life that are ready to be removed through a graceful and kind but firm approach?

- How can you open up your physical body to an even deeper understanding of your surroundings, and to connection with those you care about most?

Calling the Spirit of the Elephant

In our hectic world, we can lose sight of kindness and compassion as a daily practice. The elephant reminds us to open up our feelers, our exploring trunk, and look for moments of gentle benevolence. It might mean smiling at a stranger, or asking, "How are you holding up?" and then really listening to the response. A friend of mine recently went through a drive-up window for coffee, and when she went to pay, the cashier informed her that the car in front of her had already paid for it! She was surprised but the worker was not—she gets to be witness to these occasional random acts of generosity. Maybe you can think of an anonymous way to pass it on in a similar way.

These small gestures may seem silly and insignificant, but they have a ripple effect, raising the general level of kindness in the world. Like a daily gratitude practice, a kindness practice also strengthens your heart and mind, expanding your capacity through the gentle, caring way of the elephant.

A Prayer for Elephant Energy

Wise and soulful grandmother elephant,
let this day be a day of kindness;
let this day be a day of compassion;
let this day be a day of wisdom.
Guide me always in your great footsteps,
that I too may walk through the world
caring for others.

FOX

Teachings to Remember When Encountering Foxes

Clever and adaptable, stealthy and quick, foxes seem like magical creatures, with a wily, uncanny wildness to them. Less formidable and threatening than the bear or wolf, but just as smart and capable, the fox is often depicted as mischievous, thieving, and deceptive. Perhaps it's the wild gleam in their eye, their tendency to harass or hunt small livestock, their sharp, observant faces, or their ability to move around undetected that has built their reputation for cunning. In this way, the fox is an archetypal trickster.

Trickster wisdom can be profound, but also sometimes confusing, as it contains paradoxes and opposites.

See also: Coyote, Crow, Rabbit, Spider

Related animals: weasel, badger

Element: earth

• Stealthy, focused, and cunning
• Wild and magical
• Tricky and wise

Tricksters teach in a hidden, sideways way, and things are not always as they seem. The fox and other tricksters like the coyote and the crow appear in countless stories where they have conned someone important out of something precious, only to turn around and give it to humanity. And they aren't always the winners of their stories. Tricksters also sometimes play the fool and are humiliated, but they find a way to shrug it off and keep moving forward.

What better way to employ fox wisdom than sideways? In a tricky situation, use your creative mind to try an unexpected solution. Turning things upside down or trying on opposite perspectives can be another fox ploy. The fox is also a ready friend when you need to let go of your domestications a bit and embrace wildness in order to restore balance and flow to your life. Finally, the fox will be on your side at those annoying times when you feel duped by life. We've all had those moments. As we wallow in feelings of resentment and self-pity, the fox whispers to us from the wild places of the world: Shake yourself off, flash your toothy grin, and own up to your imperfections. After all, it's a wide, wild, imperfect world out there.

Questions to Consider

- Have you recently had an experience where you felt tricked and you're having a hard time letting it go? Can you laugh at yourself and shake it off?

- Has life been a little too sedate lately? Can you flip the script and see what happens?

- Does domestication keep you small and obedient? How might you invite some extra cunning, stealth, and focus to your life?

Calling the Spirit of the Fox

Call the energy of the fox with a daring game of "What if . . . ?" Take a few moments to jot down as many of your wildest dreams and silliest impulses as you can think of in your journal. Keep them as uncensored as possible and just let things flow. Next, pick a couple dreams or goals that jump out at you and ask yourself, "What if . . ." What if I circled the globe in a sailboat? What if I wrote to my crush? What if I signed my kid out of school for the day to go on a family adventure? Don't be afraid to embrace a certain playful edginess—you'll know what feels right to you and when you've gone too far.

This might lead to some new ideas for bringing a note of wildness into your daily routine. Have pancakes for dinner? Dye your hair purple temporarily, or permanently? Have a conversation with your cat about philosophy? This kind of silly, slightly crazy play can not only help you release a huge amount of stress, but it can also remind you that you are a strong, stealthy, clever person, ready to take on your wildest dreams and biggest challenges with a gleam in your eye and a smile on your face.

A Prayer for Fox Energy

Wild and crazy cousin fox,
slipping in and out of shadows
on the edge of the wild wood,
keep me clever and quick; help me
avoid bad tricks and traps, to see
with a sharp eye and smell with
a sharp nose. Help me keep
one foot in the wild places
and laugh when the world
gets weird.

FROG

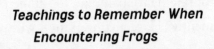

Teachings to Remember When Encountering Frogs

Frogs and toads live their lives in between two elements. Born in the water, they swim, hunt, and grow up breathing through gills, and once they mature into full-grown adults, they emerge into the air and live on land, traveling back and forth between the elements of water and earth for the rest of their lives. All frog skin can get dried out, though toads tend to be able to regulate their hydration a little better. But most of these animals need ready access to water or a humid environment.

Related animals: toad, salamander, gecko, newt

Elements: water and earth

- Abundant and nourishing
- Transformative
- Renewing

In fairy tales, frogs often symbolize ugliness, but with a hidden nobility, talent, or dignity lying just beneath. Those same fairy tales then reveal a kind of transformation, something that we can also see when we consider the frog's transition from tadpole to frog. If we consider this from the perspective of the elements, we might reflect on what it means to transform ourselves from a state in which we drift in a sea of our emotions, letting them control our destiny, until we grow the skills we need to stand on firmer ground. A healthy emotional life requires the stability of earth, with grounding in our physical body so that we know we can be secure in our present reality no matter what we're feeling moment to moment.

For the ancient Egyptians, frogs also represented abundant life, since frogs would return to Egypt every year when the Nile flooded the area with the fertile silt needed to grow food. Even today, the sound of chirping frogs in spring or summer brings to mind the abundance and ease of the season. Water is life, and everything living on earth depends on it. The health of frog populations gives us an immediate indication of the health of the water nearby. In this way, frog medicine reminds us of the fragility and importance of our water systems and brings us the sacred knowledge that physically and spiritually, we all depend on the health of our home, the earth.

Questions to Consider

- Are you in a dry spell? How could a metaphorical flood renew your life?

- Are you comfortable in two different worlds, or do you function better when you can prioritize one over the other?

Calling the Spirit of the Frog

To connect with the abundant and transformative spirit of the frog, try a water ritual. Water rituals and cleansing ceremonies have existed in innumerable cultures throughout history. We ourselves are made up of the same water that fills the oceans, drops from clouds, and runs in rivers throughout the land. Water is sacred, and we can celebrate the life-giving properties of water in simple, profound ceremony.

Here's a simple water ritual you may want to try: Consider invoking the spirit of the frog before your ceremony. You'll need a small blue bowl filled with water and something to dip into the water so that you can sprinkle it. A sprig of fresh rosemary is great for this, but you can also use a feather or a small broom. Once you have gathered your items in your space or in front of your personal altar, hold the bowl of water in your hands, close your eyes, and take a few deep breaths. Imagine all your worries and anxieties draining out of you like water, and come into the present moment. When you feel grounded and present, open your eyes and touch the surface of the water. Ask the water for its blessing and thank it for its life-giving magic. This can be as simple as saying, "Thank you for your blessings." Now take your rosemary, broom, or other implement and dip it into the water. Touch your forehead first, saying a small prayer of blessing, such as, "May I be blessed." Then sprinkle this sacred water any other place you want to bless, such as your altar, home, workspace, or the people or pets you live with.

A Prayer for Frog Energy

Little singer in the rain, friend frog,
who carries the gift of transformation
in your watery heart, help me to navigate
my emotions with a grounded mind and body;
teach me to welcome the life-giving waters
of joy and abundance.

GOAT

Teachings to Remember When Encountering Goats

Goats are fearless. Theirs is not a fearless ferocity like that of the great hunters, such as the wolf or the lion. Rather goats are fearless by way of their gifts of agility, sure-footedness, curiosity, and a determined unwillingness to stay in set boundaries if they can find any means to climb their way out.

In many ways, our contemporary culture loads us up with paralyzing fears. We know all about the countless dangers lurking around every corner. We may feel like it's foolish to take any risk or not worth the effort to try anything new. In this way, we keep ourselves small, constrained, and trapped in our own homes, hearts, and beliefs. The goat teaches that we don't need to leap into battle or defeat our enemies in order to be fearless. All we need is the curiosity and confidence to take one step at a time. In this way, step by step, we will climb higher and higher toward the top of the mountain.

Goats are the only animal of its kind (in the same family as cows, sheep, and deer) that can climb trees. On an elemental level, this affinity for heights and climbing places them simultaneously in the realms of earth and air. In this way, goats travel between the grounded stability of earth and the body, on one hand, and the heady, aspirational heights of the air on the other. For those of us who favor our body over our mind, or vice versa, the goat provides a role model of balance.

Questions to Consider

- When was the last time you tried something new? Can you set a goal to try something new this week?

- Do you feel you can find steady footing in unknown terrain? Or does fear shut you down?

- Are you feeling hemmed in? Remember, you might be much more agile and flexible than you think.

Calling the Spirit of the Goat

Like goats, humans have the ability to climb and aspire to greater heights. To connect with the goat's sense of confident freedom, consider exploring rock climbing at your local gym—or outdoors if you are lucky enough to live near the mountains. Even a satisfying climb up several flights of stairs to the top of a tall building can fulfill this urge. The climb may be arduous, but reaching the top can feel like a real accomplishment, and the change in perspective can be refreshing and cleansing.

Of course, physical climbing isn't the only way to connect with this powerful teaching. Completing a project you have put off for a long time can create the same feeling of pride, accomplishment, and balance. Just remember, like the agile goat, all you need to do is remember to take one step at a time and stay fearless.

A Prayer for Goat Energy

Nimble and curious friend goat,
Climbing ever higher, sure-footed and free,
Teach me to rise up, to try new things,
To break free of all attempts to keep my soul contained
And to dance along the mountaintops
Without fear.

GOOSE

Teachings to Remember When Encountering Geese

In one myth from ancient Egypt, the whole world was said to be birthed out of a cosmic goose egg. In other Egyptian myths, it was the sun that was born out of a goose egg laid by the earth god Geb, known as the Great Cackler. Almost all animal life springs from some kind of egg, so it makes sense that the large goose egg has become a symbol for creation itself. The goose, along with its relative the swan, is also a fiercely protective parent, and goose medicine reminds us of our common parentage with all living creatures on earth.

See also: Crane, Swan

Related animals: duck, egret, heron, pheasant

Elements: air and water

• Creative
• Instinctual
• Generous

In folklore, golden goose egg stories often warn against greed. As with all stories, Toltec shamans look into the possible domestication at work. Killing the "goose that lays the golden egg" is supposed to mean that by looking for a lot of treasure all at once, you will lose out on the daily treasure already provided to you. But perhaps the goose egg is not about material wealth, but rather creativity itself and the impulse for new life. In this case, every egg laid can be golden, or valuable, and we can remember that we can lay eggs, too: we can create with a sense of wonder and beauty, every day of our lives.

Geese and other waterfowl spend most of their lives between two places—a temperate climate during the summer and a warmer climate in the winter. Geese always know when it's time to migrate, and they lift into the air, moving into their famous V formation. As they go, their honking cries remind us that winter is not far behind. Knowing when to go is powerful goose medicine.

Domestic geese have been raised by human beings for food, and their feathers are used for writing and for bedding. It can be difficult sometimes to consider these domesticated aspects of our animal relationships, and it is part of shamanic practice to continually examine the truth of the matter for yourself. In any case, I believe that the starting place for any relationship in which we benefit from animal gifts is profound gratitude. We can honor animal life in our everyday actions and in deep spiritual and ceremonial ways as well. This is the challenge and privilege of living within an interdependent web of life. What kind of gifts are we giving back to the living world? How are we generous? What do we contribute to the web as a whole?

Questions to Consider

- Is there an aspect of your life that is coming to a natural close? What are some ways you might mark this sacred ending and honor this passing time in your life?

- Was there a time in your life when you received an unexpected gift? Did you allow yourself to receive it fully, with an open heart? How might you move that energy of generosity forward by offering a gift of your own?

Calling the Spirit of the Goose

When the season is right, see if you can catch a glimpse of a flock of geese as they wing their way to a different climate for the upcoming season. Listen to their honking cries and imagine what their journey might be like, navigating by ancestral knowledge and taking cues from the natural world. Try to imagine yourself in the body of one of these great birds high above the earth, pushed and pulled by intuition to initiate great change. We might think of our own intuition as flimsy or unreliable, but what would happen if the geese chose to ignore theirs? They would stay in a place out of season, where there is no nourishment, no warmth, and no community. When we ignore or suppress our own intuition, we might likewise be putting ourselves in mortal danger.

See if you can think of times in your own life when this lesson would have served you well. If you are grappling with a difficult change or transition, call upon the spirit of the goose to help you listen to that small voice inside. It may be telling you that now is the right time to begin a great journey toward more fertile, nourishing places.

A Prayer for Goose Energy

Cackling geese, giving birth to new
opportunities, holding the power of creation,
help me listen to my own intuition, to know
in my heart of hearts when the time is right
for me to fly.

HAWK

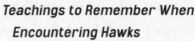

Teachings to Remember When Encountering Hawks

Hawks are among the group of exceptionally powerful spirit allies that includes bears, wolves, big cats, and even sharks. The hawk is a keen, swift hunter of deadly grace, circling overhead to get the bigger picture and then swooping down from lofty heights to snatch up its meal in the blink of an eye. It has long been a powerful symbol for those seeking wisdom and strength in times of battle or conflict. It prepares, makes a decision, and follows through on its target with resolute focus and lethal determination. Certainly, if you are looking to zero in on and accomplish a goal or next action with fierce focus, the hawk can help you do that.

But the special medicine of the hawk is also connected to its amazing eyesight. Soaring high above the earth, a hawk can spot a tiny mouse scurrying around in the brush. They also have the ability to perceive ultraviolet light in addition to the visible range of light, a kind of superpower that is thought

See also: Eagle, Owl, Vulture

Related animals: falcon, harrier, kite, kestrel, osprey

Elements: air and fire

- Visionary
- Focused
- Lucid

to increase the bird's perception of the contours and orientation of foliage and ground cover.

The hawk's domain is the mind, aligned with the element of air—the realm of mental clarity, vision, communication, and awareness. We all get mired in details sometimes and lose sight of the bigger picture. Life is complicated, and the sheer amount of input can be overwhelming. The spirit of the hawk reminds us that the best way to clear our mind is to gain some perspective. Sometimes this may even include physically moving to higher ground or open spaces, like the desert, an open plain, or a hilltop. On a windy day, it can feel as though the breeze itself is rushing through your body, blowing away all the dark, cobwebby details and revealing the stunning bigger picture. The hawk reminds us that clarity is possible, especially when we stretch out our wings and open our awareness to higher realms of consciousness.

Questions to Consider

- Can you reach for a different perspective on something that has been occupying your thoughts lately?

- Is now the time to start zeroing in on an unfinished project with the focus of the hawk?

- How can you gain more clarity in various aspects of your life? Are there mentors who can offer a fresh perspective? Can you widen your lens to include ideas you may not have thought were relevant before?

Calling the Spirit of the Hawk

A great way to seek clarity and to invoke the powerful teachings of the hawk is to perform a space clearing in your home or workspace. Through habit and repetition, our homes can easily become energetic pockets that feel stuffy and closed in. To bring in a clear perspective, begin by simply opening as many windows as you can, especially on a beautiful day with a fresh wind blowing. Let sunlight stream in. Do some practical hands-on cleaning like straightening, dusting, and vacuuming to clear the space of physical clutter and dirt.

Once you've opened up the room a bit, you can enhance this expansive feeling of newness even more by playing some light music that lifts your heart. If you sing or play an instrument or a drum, these are great ways to clear and lighten energy as well. You may want to burn some incense or use essential oil sprays to freshen the scent in the room. As you lighten your space, thank the hawk for bringing inner and outer clarity into your life.

As you update your space, you might also consider adding something that reminds you that a change in perspective and scale is a powerful healing tool. A map or globe, a magnifying glass, objects or representations in miniature, or artwork that depicts an aerial view might all do the trick.

A Prayer for Hawk Energy

Keen-eyed friend, soaring on
wings of light through the high clean air,
share your gift of insight with me; help me
cut through the clutter in my heart,
and begin this new day with
a fresh spirit.

HIPPOPOTAMUS

See also: Elephant, Whale

Related animals: manatee, rhinoceros

Elements: earth and water

- Allowing
- Calm and assertive
- Protective and nurturing

Teachings to Remember When Encountering Hippos

Hippos can be found in large herds, grazing near and lazing through Africa's many rivers, lakes, and swamps. All along the Nile, great hippos tiptoe along the riverbed, their bulk carried in the river's gentle current and only the mounds of backs and the tops of their heads visible above the waterline. The ancient Egyptians honored this fierce and impressive animal in the form of the hippo-headed goddess Taweret, the patron of protection, childbirth, and child-rearing. Female hippos are indeed fearsome and nurturing protectors of their young. While hippos are herbivores and may seem slow and gentle as they munch on up to one hundred pounds of grass on a nightly basis, they are also notably aggressive and territorial. They can outrun a human on their stumpy legs and have jaws with sharp incisors powerful enough to kill a ten-foot crocodile. The bellow of a bull hippo is as loud as the roar of a lion.

Hippo moves through the water as gracefully as a dancer, supported by the element in which they spend most of their time. This lightness and buoyancy contrast with the sturdy athleticism the hippo needs on land to climb steep riverbanks and seek out fresh grass to eat. All of us can feel heavy and weighed down in certain moments. We're low on motivation, or we feel like everything is ten times harder than it needs to be.

What if you went to the metaphorical water and allowed yourself to be held up and supported for a while? Needing help, asking for assistance, and accepting support can be difficult for us as individuals. Trusting others with the weight of our true selves and our problems can feel bothersome or even dangerous. We may feel stronger and more capable when we muscle through and try to go it alone, but this is a recipe for burnout and resentment. Furthermore, if you are willing to help others but don't believe you are worthy of help yourself, this may be a reflection of a degraded sense of self-worth. Everyone deserves to delegate, relax, and trust.

Remembering that water is the symbol for emotional flow, we can also learn to be supported by our emotions rather than ruled by them. One common agreement from childhood teaches that we can't trust our emotional selves—this often comes from a parent or teacher telling us to stop crying or saying we have to calm down. But if we learn to work with our emotions, to float and move gracefully in and among them and allow them to support us in our work in the world, we may find we have a much healthier relationship with our inner selves.

Hippos live primarily in calm waters and spend much of their lives submerged in these peaceful places. Yet they also choose their moments to aggressively ward off intruders or open their mouths in a wide yawn to say, "Keep away from my baby!" In our own lives, it's worth examining how we might calm our watery emotional body through meditation, prayer, deep breathing, journaling, and other mindfulness practices. This doesn't mean we abandon the important work of creating strong boundaries and defending what we care about. Sometimes we mistake mindfulness with weakness, but the truth is that if you are present and grounded, feeling supported by your emotions rather than being ruled by them, and move through the world with a peaceful sense of inner equilibrium, you are much better able to handle conflict and protect what's truly important when the situation calls for it.

Questions to Consider

- What are you being called to nurture and protect in your life right now?

- Check in with your emotional body. What is it crying out for? What might you do to soothe and rebalance your emotional wellness?

- Is there someone close to you who can help support you right now? What else best supports you? A clean and well-organized space? Healthy food? Good sleep hygiene?

Calling the Spirit of the Hippo

The soothing properties of water can calm heated emotions and bring relief to your emotional body. Whenever you can, spending the day in a natural body of water can bring deep relaxation to your spirit through the combination of earth, water, fresh air, and the sun. But even when you don't have the time or resources to spend all day in a natural spring or at the beach, you can take advantage of water's healing energy and connect with the balancing and buoyant wisdom of the hippo, by taking regular healing baths.

Bringing a sense of ritual to your baths can add emotional and spiritual cleansing to your physical practice of getting clean. You can add herbs, essential oils, or other bath products to enhance the relaxing atmosphere. Try playing soothing and powerful music, lighting candles, and spending your bath time in meditation and prayer, allowing yourself to trust the healing and calming power of the water to wash away your stress from the day. Let the water support you, and in your mind's eye imagine that you are floating in a great flowing river, held up by the hands of Mother Earth.

A Prayer for Hippo Energy

Great hippopotamus, wise mother
buoyed by the calm, watery gifts of earth,
teach me how to balance fierceness with peace,
and help me find the strength to let myself be supported
and held by others, so that I can protect those around me, including
myself, with a mindful heart and a gentle spirit.

HORSE

See also: Deer

Related animals: donkey, elk, mule, reindeer

Elements: earth and air

- Free, balanced, and swift
- Cooperative
- Proud and noble

Teachings to Remember When Encountering Horses

Horses have been the backbone of human endeavor and the subject of art, religion, and adoration for thousands of years, with the first archaeological evidence of humans and horses working together dating back to at least 3500 BCE. Most horses today are domesticated, but there are still a few wild horses left in the world. Horses have been a vital part of our lives in areas of transportation, farming, hunting, and building, as well as more problematic elements of human society, such as gambling and war. It's difficult to argue with those who claim that horses are just as responsible for our civilization as humans are.

Horses are the basis for several majestic mythological animals as well, such as Pegasus, the hippogriff, and the unicorn. Tibetan spirituality associates the mythological wind horse with the human soul and holds it as a sign of good fortune.

Horses are known for their speed as well as their stamina. They can be fierce fighters and courageous allies, and their quiet strength and the sense of freedom achieved by riding horses have been used for therapeutic purposes in recent years. Horses seem to be able to see inside you, intuiting your inner state and responding to you on a soul level. The emotional bond that can form between a horse and a human being is legendary, and for many people this bond is a sacred part of their life's journey and brings a sense of purpose and wholeness.

Horse domestication can offer clues to our own. While a horse can be "broken" through violence and control, there is a much more powerful way to work with the horse, in a spirit of gentle collaboration and mutual strength. Our own domestication, in the Toltec sense of the word, is similar. We are often taught how to behave or what to believe in ways that go against our inner nature. We can work with ourselves to replace that domestication with a sense of genuine curiosity, love, self-respect, and openness.

Questions to Consider

- When do you feel most free? What actions can you take today to reinvigorate a feeling of balance and freedom?

- What has been your most intimate collaboration with another being—human or animal? Did it reveal your inner self to you in ways you didn't expect?

- Do you understand that you are a creature of nobility and purpose? Can you call on the horse to share these attributes with you?

Calling the Spirit of the Horse

If you are fortunate enough to have the means to interact with horses on a regular basis, then you already know how much we have to learn from this amazing animal. Working with horses directly can be a humbling experience, as the most rewarding working relationship with horses takes patience, respect, and kindness. Consider how this might influence your relationships with other human beings, as well as with yourself.

If you have not yet worked with horses but feel drawn to do so, reach out and see if there are any stables in your area that offer riding lessons or that might be looking for help tending to the horses there. You can often learn a lot about yourself by mucking out stalls, feeding horses, or currying their coats. Be sure to do some research to make sure the place you choose treats its horses with dignity and care. There may also be organizations in your area that work to protect horses from mistreatment, and getting involved with one of these organizations can be another way to reach out to the spirit of the horse on your spiritual journey.

A Prayer for Horse Energy

Noble horse, proud and swift,
help me to find my own wild strength,
to work in cooperation with all creatures,
to achieve balance and wholeness
so that I might run with the wind toward
my highest calling.

HUMMINGBIRD

Teachings to Remember When Encountering Hummingbirds

Hummingbirds zip around like flying jewels, stopping and hovering and even flying backward. Colorful, iridescent plumage catches and reflects a rainbow of light. Their bright, glittering pigment, speed, and agility make them seem almost otherworldly, as though sprites and fairies were coming to visit. We hold still and marvel when a hummingbird comes into view—and it's as though time stops in that moment, suspended in a delicious, enchanted present. While hummingbirds' main sustenance comes from eating bugs, they are always on the move, looking for the sweet nectar that fuels their incredible bursts of energy and the movement of their wings, which is so fast the human eye can only read it as a blur. Their extraordinarily high metabolism enables them to convert nectar into instant energy.

The hummingbird teaches us how to seek out and suck in the energy stores of creativity, color, and joy all around us. When we get stuck in our everyday routine and feel weighed down by our responsibilities, the hummingbird reminds us of the vibrancy of doing things quickly and lightly, with purpose. By calling upon the small, powerful spirit of the hummingbird, you can revitalize and reinvigorate your life with bright, vivacious energy. What's more, this energy is infectious, and will draw others to you as though to a sparkling jewel.

See also: Dragonfly, Butterfly, Peacock

Related animals: splendid fairy wren, starling, swallow

Element: air

- Energetic and vital
- Expressive
- Live-giving

Questions to Consider

- What part of your life can you hold up to the sunlight today and watch it shine in all of its diversity, radiance, and color?

- Where can you go to find the most accessible sweetness right now, the energizing burst of inspiration you need to take your creativity to the next level?

Calling the Spirit of the Hummingbird

You may already have your backyard set up to attract hummingbirds or know someone who does. If not, consider hanging a feeder in your yard or planting native plants that attract butterflies and hummingbirds. When they come to visit, pause and take them in for however long they stay.

Another way of calling the vital, energetic spirit of the hummingbird into your life is to find some way to enhance your day with color, light, sound, art, or anything else that lifts your heart and makes you move a little faster. It's easy to get bogged down in our routines—consider taking yourself out for what creativity author Julia Cameron calls an artist date. Go to a local museum, attend a concert at an unusual venue, or just take a walk in an area you don't visit often. By stepping out of your normal routine, you may find yourself refreshed and inspired to tackle your projects with renewed vigor. Another way to concretize the power of the hummingbird is through your wardrobe, jewelry, and/or accessories. Even small pieces that reflect light, shimmer, or pop with color can bring your day to life and inspire those around you as well.

A Prayer for Hummingbird Energy

Bright jewel, sister hummingbird, who dances
in and out of the air like a flashing diamond,
help me bring light, freshness, air, joy, and color
into my heart's home, so that I may find a renewed
energy, fire, and creative spark in my life.

JAGUAR

See also: Cat, Lion

Related animals: bobcat, cheetah, cougar, leopard, lynx, mountain lion, tiger

Element: earth

- Focused and intent
- Aware
- Driven

Teachings to Remember When Encountering Jaguars

The jaguar, the largest native cat in the Americas, stalks through many Native American cultures, including the Maya, Aztec, and Toltec. Jaguar warriors, called *ocelotl* in Nahuatl, were an elite fighting class during the height of the Aztec civilization; they believed that during battle they would be infused with the strength of the jaguar. The jaguar was also sacred to the Aztec god Tezcatlipoca, who was associated with night, obsidian, beauty, and war.

People wage war and battle for control and suppression, often as a result of an unexamined collective dream that is really about something else, such as fear. But there is another—a spiritual—aspect to the idea of war—and in fact in my family we are called Toltec warriors. We do not wage political wars, but this name reminds us that what we are doing takes discipline, persistence, and a willingness to be in conflict with our domesticated past and certain aspects of the Dream of the Planet. It is an ongoing, inward battle of revealing our true selves, staying true to our word, and remaining connected to the life force within us.

In this way, the cunning and determination of large cats and other major predators can be powerful allies in this fight. Jaguar energy commands respect, and it takes skill and practice to work with it. Skilled warriors know that becoming distracted can mean the difference between life and death, so they learn how to focus everything they have into the present moment. Even when the stakes are not as high, the jaguar medicine teaches us how to draw ourselves away from any distraction and focus on our present goal. In its stillness and presence, the jaguar opens its senses and takes in everything it can perceive with its senses.

In addition to cultivating this intense awareness, the jaguar embodies decisive action in the present moment. When stalking its prey, the jaguar holds intent and power—a being of pure focus. Whenever I feel I need to draw all my energy toward a single goal, or I want to move forward on something but my doubts and fears are holding me back, I call on the jaguar to help me be strong, fearless, and capable. The jaguar teaches me that I can manifest my dreams by taking charge of every moment of my life, by practicing focus and honing my intent. If I wait and question each move that I make, if I waste time and agonize over every little thing, I may lose my chance to attain my heart's desire. Jaguar teaches us how to see the right moment to launch ourselves forward and achieve our goals.

Questions to Consider

- How can warrior energy bring strength and focus to your deepest intent?

- What part of your life would benefit right now from strong, decisive action?

• What happens when you use your physical senses to increase your awareness? Does this increase your distraction or sharpen your focus?

Calling the Spirit of the Jaguar

Silent meditation builds your capacity for awareness and focus. This may seem counterintuitive when it comes to the jaguar. The jaguar is a powerful hunting animal, and warrior energy is all about fighting, right? No. The jaguar's gifts for hunting lie in its stealthy, intense focus, which we can build up in ourselves by sitting in stillness and silence, paying attention to the breath, and learning how to be in the present moment.

If there's a goal or dream you have been working on, call upon the spirit of the jaguar before you begin your meditation, and then find a single word that encompasses your goal. As you inhale, imagine you are breathing in a golden light that flows to your solar plexus; as you exhale, see your word in your inner mind, and imagine the golden light moving out with your breath and surrounding your goal. If thoughts or emotions arise that are not in keeping with your focus, just let them fall away naturally. Meditation isn't an easy practice, but with time and attention you can learn to narrow your focus to a single purpose, like a jaguar seeking its prey.

A Prayer for Jaguar Energy

Powerful one, jaguar in the shadows,
help me hone my focus so that it is as
sharp as an obsidian knife or a wild cat's claw.
Make me into the perfect hunter of my heart's desire.

JELLYFISH

Teachings to Remember When Encountering Jellyfish

Translucent, silent, and strange, delicate and deadly, jellyfish float through the vast oceans like alien seaflowers. They teach us about the strength of diversity and beauty and the willingness to go with the flow. Having evolved into a wide and fascinating array of shapes, colors, and sizes, even their names seem to read like poetry: moon jelly, flower hat jelly, lion's mane jelly, crystal jelly, red paper lantern jelly, bloodybelly comb jelly, black sea nettle, fried egg jelly, coronate medusa, pink meanie, by-the-wind sailor, cannonball jelly, cauliflower jelly, and the list goes on. We have only catalogued a fraction of the diverse types of jellyfish, and marine scientists think there may well be hundreds of thousands more species we've never even seen. I highly recommend spending some time watching a live jellyfish cam via an aquarium. Take a few minutes to bask in the peaceful drift of living poetry, or put it on your screen in the background to bring calm and inspiration to your space.

All jellyfish are members of the subphylum Medusozoa, which derives its name

Related animals: coral, sea anemone

Element: water

• Poetic
• Luminous
• Creative

from the Greek legend of Medusa, whose hair was a nest of poisonous vipers. Many jellyfish have stinging cells in their long, hairlike tentacles that can inflict severe pain and occasionally death on contact. This double edge quality is a part of jellyfish medicine: that immense and amazing beauty is combined with the need to be deeply respectful of boundaries is a teaching in and of itself—a teaching from the whole Mother Earth.

Additionally, about half of known jellyfish are bioluminescent, meaning they glow in the dark. This natural glow offers a decoy against predators, attracts and mesmerizes prey, or helps animals communicate. Even without bioluminescence we all have an inner radiance, and our thoughts and actions make it shine out into the world.

Questions to Consider

- What's the light you shine in the world? What can you do to make it shine even brighter?

- How do you communicate beauty to others? Dance, music, poetry, organization, community?

- Where do you see diversity expressed in your personal life, and how can you enhance it?

Calling the Spirit of the Jellyfish

A wonderful way to get in touch with the beauty and creative grace of jellyfish is to dive into poetry. If you think of poetry as being difficult to understand or intimidating to write, remember that this is simply a belief you picked up somewhere along the way. It doesn't have to be true for you. A simple way to begin to appreciate the beauty of poetry is to read and write haiku. One format for this simple but profound Japanese poetic form, as you may know, is a poem comprised of three lines only, each with a specific syllable count: five syllables in the first line, seven in the second line, and five in the final line. Traditionally, haiku focus on the natural world. Strict parameters like these can actually sometimes help get our creativity flowing, but if you're inspired to break out of this mold, that's great too.

You might take inspiration from a jellyfish live cam, as I mentioned, and try to write a haiku based on watching these creatures float across your screen for a few minutes. As you do, take several deep, relaxing breaths, letting go of any tension from your day. Allow words to come freely to your mind as you watch them, jotting down whatever arises for you. Then, when you're ready, see if you can draw out an observation or emotion from your experience, and fit that into a few short sentences of a haiku.

A Prayer for Jellyfish Energy

Seaflower jelly
poetry of ocean deep
pulsing inner light

Alien beauty
delicate glow from the dark
calm ocean heartbeat

KOMODO DRAGON

See also: Alligator

Related animals: crocodile, dinosaur, Gila monster, giant tegu, goanna, monitor lizard

Element: fire

- Primal
- Imaginative
- Ancient

Teachings to Remember When Encountering Komodo Dragons

Komodo dragons are the largest lizards on earth, weighing up to 150 pounds. They are fierce predators, with intimidating teeth and long forked tongues, and their tail is as long as their body. Their skin is covered in armored scales, and scientists think they have a venomous bite that puts their prey into shock and renders them incapable of fleeing or fighting back. These creatures of formidable instinct and deadly focus remind us that we too can use our instincts to hone our intention with forceful determination.

The Komodo dragons living in Indonesia are as close to living, breathing dragons as you can get on planet earth. The only thing that would make these magnificent lizards something straight out of myth and legend would be the ability to breathe fire and to fly on a pair of great, leathery wings.

Dragons, as mythological creatures, have fascinated humans for centuries. While they're always depicted as powerful, the European stories describe evil, fire-breathing creatures who guard hordes of treasure, and in Eastern traditions dragons tend to have auspicious powers over the elements and are bearers of good luck and success. While this is a book exploring animals that exist right now on the planet, there is wisdom in considering the meaning and mystery of mythological creatures. Dragon wisdom can breathe creative fire into our projects and goals or help us fiercely guard the treasure in our own lives—the people, things, and ideals we consider priceless and worth protecting at all costs.

Komodo dragons, the earthly lizards, are tied to an ancient evolutionary lineage that calls to mind the dinosaurs who roamed the earth long before us. Like dragonflies, cuttlefish, and other animals that have retained their form and function for millennia, lizards remind us that all living creatures exist in a tiny sliver of time on a very, very old planet. Thinking of the many millions of species that have lived and died can fill us with wonder and awe and give us a healthy sense of our smallness and how precious and fleeting our lives are. Meditating on the meaning of deep time in this way has the power to inspire and humble us.

Questions to Consider

- How can you honor your intuition and instincts about a situation or question that's been on your mind?

- What gifts might a broader perspective give to you right now?

- What treasures are you protecting and why? Are you are holding on to things that you could let go of to better protect other treasures?

Calling the Spirit of the Komodo Dragon

Children and adults alike love to immerse themselves in realms of fantasy, imagination, mythology, and fairy tales. The popularity of books, movies, and television shows such as *The Lord of the Rings* and *Game of Thrones* prove that dragons still light our collective creative spark. A great way to tap into this energy is through storytelling.

Stories are as old as human beings. While in-person oral storytelling is no longer our main entertainment option in the way it once was, stories still have a unique power to captivate people. You may already be familiar with some of the more popular storytelling podcasts and events, such as The Moth or other story slams. Local storytelling guilds, events, and festivals provide another forum for sharing this talent. Call on the powerful creative fire of the Komodo dragon and his fictional cousins by learning more about the art of telling stories, and settle in regularly to listen as other people share theirs.

A Prayer for Komodo Dragon Energy

Mighty Komodo dragon, earthly cousin
to the great dragons of myth and legend,
fill me with inspiration and fiery illumination,
with awe, humility, and wonder at the vast reaches
of time, the immensity of life, and the
amazing wealth of Mother Earth.

LION

See also: Cat, Jaguar

Related animals: bobcat, cheetah, cougar, leopard, lynx, mountain lion, tiger

Elements: earth and fire

- Noble
- Vocal
- Powerful and courageous

Teachings to Remember When Encountering Lions
Lions, with their beautiful golden manes and graceful strength, are a symbol of power, leadership, and fierceness in many ancient and contemporary societies. They have long been associated with royalty, and because of their golden eyes and coat, as well as the male's impressive mane reminiscent of the sun's rays, lions have often been associated with the sun. Ancient Egyptians, for example, worshipped a number of goddesses that were depicted as lions and associated with the sun, such as the fierce goddess Sekhmet, daughter of the sun god Ra, who was depicted with the body of a woman and the head of a lion.

Strong and agile hunters, they are capable of shocking bursts of speed, often coordinating their hunt in social groups under the cover of darkness. We think of them as unstoppable predators, keepers of balance, and while they certainly are a formidable predator, they are successful only around a quarter of the time. They are not above claiming prey that smaller hunters have killed, which might also contribute to their kingly status. Plus, they tend to conserve energy for their hunts by napping away much of the day, much like a house cat.

Naturally, the lion's regal nature, strength, and physical power have made it an emblem of kingship and leadership the world over. In addition, sculptures of lions are found at the entrance to many ancient temples or are depicted as accompanying deities as companions and guardians. A successful leader, in the spirit of the great lion, employs great courage and strength but also fulfills their obligation to protect those that have been entrusted into their care. Being a leader of integrity and honor means guarding those we love against harm, or even ourselves. This goes beyond physical protection; we must guard our heart and soul against illusions or even against our own unwise decisions, and the fierce teachings of the lion can help us do just that.

Because of their spiritual association with the sun, and therefore with heat and light, the lion occupies the realms of both earth and fire on the medicine wheel. Fire is the element of creativity, passion, joy, and determination. Lion medicine can renew the fiery creative spirit within, as well as help you find or re-energize your authentic creative voice and the passion to share your work with the world. The lion's mighty roar, after all, can be heard over a distance of five miles. The next time you are preparing to promote your work, or need a boost of energy for your current project, imagine being filled with the invigorating roar of the lion.

Apex predators are thought to be in charge of their food web and territories, which may feel like meaningful animal medicine when you are looking for support in a leadership role or as you claim your authority over your own destiny. On the other hand, you may be more interested in the lion's protective instincts, matrilineal family dynamics, or the symbolic power of their roar. As the artist of your own life, you get to choose what is true for you.

Questions to Remember

- How do you protect what you love? What additional ways might you claim your own power and amplify your courage?

• What is your equivalent of the "lion's roar"? How does your creativity express itself in your life? How can you own it fiercely and proudly?

Calling the Spirit of the Lion

If you are feeling stuck and want to invoke the lion's fierce creativity in your life, consider beginning your creative practice with a little yoga. Lion's pose, or Simhasana in Sanskrit, is said to help release stress and relax the muscles of the face and neck, as well as helping to fill the lungs with fresh oxygen. Even if you are not a regular practitioner of yoga, this simple pose is easy to perform. You can sit cross-legged, on your knees, or on all fours. If your position allows it, spread your hands wide, like claws. The pose is activated when you align and lengthen your spine, open your eyes wide looking upward, open your mouth as wide as possible, and extend your tongue down to your chin as far as you can; then exhale a long "haaaaa" and imagine you are breathing out a mighty, creative fire that fills the room with creativity. You may even want to practice a few good roars as you do this pose.

A Prayer for Lion Energy

Great king lion, golden eye of the sun,
help me to be a faithful guardian of those I love,
as well as of my own inner being. Teach me
your graceful leadership; may I be set alight
with the fire of creativity and the vital roar
of a life filled with authentic passion.

MOLE

Teachings to Remember When Encountering Moles

Moles dig under the surface, mostly blind but "seeing" with their feet and noses, creating vast tunnels and burrows whose every contour they know. Their burrows annoy many proud homeowners who prefer a pristine lawn over a field of lumpy molehills, yet their diligent digging aerates the soil and keeps it healthy. One of the only mammals that lives almost entirely underground, they sense and smell everything around them in search of earthworms to eat. When a worm falls into one of its tunnels, the mole senses the vibration and heads straight to it. Highly sensitive to the space around them, moles connect deeply to their home in the earth.

See also: Earthworm, Cicada

Related animals: armadillo, hedgehog, mole rat, shrew

Element: earth

- Stable
- Grounded
- Spacially aware

In this way, moles teach us a great deal about awareness and grounding. Human beings have a sense associated with instinctively "knowing" where our body is in the space surrounding us; it's called proprioception, and it's the reason why you can close your eyes and move your hand to touch your opposing elbow. This sense helps us navigate through life without constantly bumping into things, though we can be distracted from this sense if we are preoccupied or inebriated. We can also develop this sense, as athletes or dancers do, through intentional, focused movement. On a wider symbolic level, body awareness relates to our sense of self not only as a physical being, but on a mental and spiritual level as well. Mole medicine helps us dig deeper into physical, emotional, and spiritual stability.

In addition, moles can teach us about "grounding," not only because they live underground, but because they are in tune with the earth in a very concrete way. Being attuned to the earth around them keeps them safe and well fed. Humans also require a profound connection to the earth we live on. Many of us have lost this critical sense of connection. Part of this is external—in our homes, cities, and places of work we rarely come into physical contact with the actual soil beneath our feet. Part of it is internal—we are distracted by demanding jobs, social lives, and the constant stream of information beamed into our phones and computers, always pulling us away from our grounded connection to the earth. Like body awareness, we can develop our ability to ground our energy and reconnect with the vast, solid, and loving presence of Mother Earth. We can regain our balance and build our awareness of what's really going on around us and what really needs our true attention.

Questions to Consider

- What can you do today to make yourself feel like you are on firmer ground—physically, emotionally, and spiritually?

- Are you distracted by your surroundings? What would it take to tunnel down into what really matters? Time away from devices? A walk in nature?

- What would happen if you closed your eyes and tried to see the solution to a problem with your body instead of your eyes?

Calling the Spirit of the Mole

To connect with the spirit of the mole, and the energy of the earth, try this basic grounding exercise:

Go outside somewhere you can be safe and undisturbed for at least twenty minutes. Take off your shoes and stand comfortably in a place where your bare feet are in contact with the earth. Close your eyes and take a few slow, deep breaths. Then, as you continue to breathe, spend a few moments just listening to the sounds around you: birds, the wind in the trees or the grass, traffic, airplanes. See if you can extend your hearing out to include sounds you hadn't noticed before. Then do the same with your sense of smell: the grass, exhaust from a passing car, the heat rising up from the concrete, flowers. Finally, extend your sense of touch; become aware of any wind on your skin or in your hair. Once you have expanded into your senses, really plant your feet into the ground, feeling the exact spot that you meet the earth in this moment. Imagine great roots extending down from the soles of your feet into the deep core of the planet. As you breathe, the energy of the earth rises up through these roots into your body like nourishing sap, then spills out into the air like the limbs of a tree through your head and your hands.

Stay like this for a while, feeling the energy of the earth, the open awareness of your senses, and your rootedness in the ground. Then, when you are ready, place your hands down on the ground and let the energy sink back into the earth, along with any worries or other distractions you want to let go of. Know that you are connected to the earth, deeply rooted in place at all times, even when you can't feel it. Take several breaths and come back to your awareness, and say a thankful prayer to the spirit of the mole for teaching you the wisdom of grounding.

A Prayer for Mole Energy

Brother mole, digger in the dark,
keeper of the earth's great energies,
teach me to be in connection with
Mother Earth at all times, to be aware
in this present time and space, to know
what is important, to know
what is real.

MONKEY

Teachings to Remember When Encountering Monkeys

Monkeys are our nearest relatives in the animal world, and humans have long expressed our close kinship by depicting them in religion, spirituality, and folklore. Clever and curious, with busy minds, hands, and tails, monkeys move across and through all kinds of terrain, living in social groups. The Hindu god Hanuman is a monkey god of strength and courage and also associated with wrestling and acrobatics. The agility and energy of monkeys are thrilling to watch, and a kind of whirling chaos seems to spread wherever monkeys go—delightful and exhausting. I imagine this is the origin of the Buddhist term *monkey mind*, which we can intuitively understand as restlessness and the inability to control or calm our thoughts.

> **Related animals:** ape, baboon, gibbon, gorilla, lemur, macaque, tarsier
>
> **Element:** earth
>
> • Creative
> • Jovial
> • Energetic, agile, and expressive

Movement is one of those gifts we tend overlook until our capacity is diminished. Most of us will be injured at some point, or if we're lucky to live into old age our mobility may change. In my view, we can cultivate gratitude for our body in any state, and relish all it can accomplish. When we are living with a disability, which happens to all of us at one point or another, ingenious monkey medicine can think up new ways of moving that support and embrace our differences.

The monkey leaps and dances within the earth quadrant of the medicine wheel, associated with the body. Western thinking tends to separate body and mind, but the monkey's mind seems to inhabit and animate every inch of its body. This is true for us too, even if we've forgotten it. For this reason, we need to move not only to stay healthy but to strengthen and refresh our emotional capacities and our creative expression as well. Creativity belongs to everyone, not only artists, and ingenious ideas and breakthroughs have come to bodies in motion. Whether you're dancing, walking, hiking, doing acrobatics, or practicing yoga, movement fills your body with energy and connects you to the living energy of the organic world. How could it be any other way? Your body is, after all, a purely organic being. You can't help but be connected to the earth when you are fully connected to your body.

Questions to Consider

- Can you find some humor in a rough situation?

- When's the last time you jumped around and danced for no reason or took at quick spin around the block?

- What does a creative body look like to you? How does it move? What could it explore?

Calling the Spirit of the Monkey

Playing games, especially physical ones like Simon Says or charades, can invite positive monkey energy, as can dancing of any kind. Monkeys teach us that laughter is the best medicine. Their wild and mischievous antics can be enchanting, and watching them in the wild or in a zoo can get us laughing fast.

Laughing, like movement, can be healing emotionally and physically and can fortify social bonds and relieve loneliness.

There are even laughing groups, laughing exercises, and laughing yoga! A friend of mine once attended a laughter session where a group of people performed various exercises designed to inspire laughter. She told me it seemed silly at first, with everyone in the room nervous and embarrassed to be walking around pretending to laugh as they shook each other's hands. However, laughter is irresistible for the body, and what seemed like fake, awkward laughter gave way to the real thing as everyone committed to the absurdity of the situation. Within a couple of minutes, everyone was laughing, and when the session was over, everyone felt energized, refreshed, and happy. It was as though a fog had lifted from the room, and my friend felt like she was physically and emotionally lighter and more connected than before.

When you are laughing, feeling free and alive, the spirit of the monkey is with you.

A Prayer for Monkey Energy

Cousin monkey, being of pure energy,
agility, and ingenuity, help me
to take time out of every day to be
grateful for this amazing body, made
of the living earth, and for the power
of laughter to lighten souls and make new friends.

MOTH

See also: Butterfly, Owl

Related animals: silkworm

Elements: air and earth

- Optimistic
- Reverential
- Beautiful

Teachings to Remember When Encountering Moths

Moth moves unseen through the night on paper wings, in love with the moon and the flickering flame of a candle. She tells the ancient stories of loss, of remembrance, of impermanence. Like the butterfly, the moth is a transformational creature, starting as a caterpillar and emerging into the air on the lightest of wings. Moths share the butterfly's beauty, though we don't always notice it, and they can have stunning markings, such as those on the Madagascan sunset moth or the polyphemus moth, and be tiny, flitting creatures or as massive as the great Atlas moth, which can be larger than a human hand. In their caterpillar stage, moths and butterflies are creatures close to the earth, and in this form one species of moth produces silk, which humans have used to create beautiful fabric for thousands of years.

Most moths are nocturnal, and many perform important roles as pollinators of plants whose blossoms open at night. Being night creatures, moths have long been associated with the moon and candlelight, as well as more frightening concepts, such as death and ghosts. Moths do appear ghostlike, winging silently in the darkness, illuminated briefly by light and seeming to glow. Some species of moth have been said to be messengers of impending death or memory loss. This is good example of an opportunity to look more closely at the domesticated story of the moth and find out what is true for you.

We don't know why moths are drawn to light, but through their fragile beauty and this willingness to seek out light in the dark, I see the moth's teaching to encompass beauty, silence, and reverence for light, all within the context of darkness. There is always light, goodness, and beauty to be found even in dark times. Death is a part of life, and we can approach it with respect and reverence instead of fear. We can even see the beauty in it. The moth teaches us to make our hearts light and soft in times of darkness and to keep looking for the light.

Questions to Consider

- When have you felt most in the dark? What points of light did you reach out for during that time?

- Can you hold the thought of loss or death with gentle reverence, light as the wings of the moth?

- Have you taken time recently to thank your ancestors—whether they are related to you or are ancestors of spirit—for the beautiful gifts they've bestowed on you in this lifetime?

Calling the Spirit of the Moth

Connecting with the spirit of the moth and its quest to seek the light is as simple as stepping outside on a summer night and turning to face the moon.

Try to find someplace quiet, perhaps when the moon's light is obscured by clouds. It shouldn't take long for you to notice moths fluttering around a nearby light source, such as a porch light. If possible, turn the light off, and open your senses out into the night. Imagine the night alive with the scent of open blooms, full of nectar. You are surrounded by beauty even in darkness, even when it may be hidden.

Wait for the moon to come out from behind the clouds and turn your face toward the light. If you've been experiencing a particularly difficult time, a dark night of the soul, ask the moon's gentle light for guidance.

A Prayer for Moth Energy

Moth light, moonlight,
hold me in the hush and silence
of the night—help me find a guiding
star in the darkness, help me see
that I am surrounded by beauty
even when all the light goes out.

NIGHTINGALE

Teachings to Remember When Encountering Nightingales

In the sweet-smelling night all over Europe and parts of Africa, the air vibrates with the trills, clicks, and swooping song of the nightingale. Though they don't live in the Americas, nightingales play starring roles in so many fairy tales, songs, and poems that many in this part of the world have heard their story and have a sense of their importance. In Hans Christian Andersen's "The Nightingale," for example, the sweet song of the nightingale charms Death itself, who spares the life of the emperor of China.

Nightingales have a plain and simple appearance; yet their intricate song is one of the most beautiful sounds in the world. In this way, the nightingale reflects the strength and beauty of the inner self. It's easy to get caught up in appearances, but the nightingale reminds us to do the deeper work of cultivating and maintaining our inner song—our authentic and truest self. Music has long been associated with the soul, so it's only natural that we connect the idea of a robust, soulful, inner life with the beautiful and uplifting song of the nightingale.

Related animals: black rail, canary, lark, mockingbird, oriole, tanager, thrush, whip-poor-will, wren

Element: air

• Uplifting
• Conscientious
• Healing

True to its name, the nightingale sings at night as well as during the day. This adds another dimension to this bird's teachings. On a sunny day when things are going our way, we may find that it's much easier to maintain a healthy sense of self and spiritual equilibrium. But if we can sing through the darker, more difficult times, drawing on our inner strength and authentic self, our song becomes all the sweeter. In the face of personal and global challenges, we can sing to bring about our own healing and the healing of others as well.

Questions to Consider

- If you've found yourself moving through a dark time in your life, can you find the strength to sing? What would that look like for you?

- Have you been fixated on your physical self lately? How might you turn to your inner self and do some reflection there as well?

Calling the Spirit of Nightingale

Music entwines with spirit. The Greek philosopher Pythagoras had a theory that the "music of the spheres" lies at the heart of the universe; today, we enjoy Gregorian chant, Gospel music, drum circles, and pop music. Music gives voice to human experience across all cultural, theological, and philosophical boundaries. Music unites people.

To connect to the powerful spirit of the nightingale, consider adding music to your regular spiritual practice. This might be through creating a special meditation or ritual playlist that helps elevate your consciousness, playing an instrument, singing, or chanting on a regular basis. Let go of the expectation of performance or perfection—the point here is to connect with your innermost self through breath, sound, and feeling. The spirit of the nightingale will be with you as you allow your soul to pour forth from the core of your being. Your heartsong is unique to you, beautiful just as it is. Singing or making music with others is another way to expand your practice and deepen your interpersonal bonds. Joining a band, community choir, instrumental ensemble, chanting group, or sing-along is a great way to share music-making with others.

A Prayer for Nightingale Energy

Sister nightingale, singer of the song of life
even in the midst of darkness, teach me
how to open my heart and let the
soul song of my authentic self
ring out through all aspects of my life.

OPOSSUM

Related animals: armadillo, hedgehog, mongoose, porcupine, Tasmanian devil, wombat

Element: earth

- Resourceful
- Adaptable
- Self-reliant

Teachings to Remember When Encountering Opossums

The opossum wanders on the sidelines, a contented loner, waddling through the dark finding its next meal with its nose. These marsupials don't make long-term nests or burrows and don't hang out with others of their kind after they leave their mother's pouch. They have adapted to a wide range of environments and can eat almost anything. You may have seen one on a walk at night, or glimpsed its reflective yellow eyes in your car's headlights. With a pointed face, sharp teeth, large five-fingered feet, and a long rat tail, an opossum can be startling. They might even hiss at you. Like most of us, however, the opossum is pretty docile when left alone. One of the most powerful aspects of their animal medicine is that they are great and ingenious survivors—so much so that they predate and have outlasted many of the planet's mammal species.

The opossum's most famous survival tool is playing dead, or "playing possum." A threatened opossum will instinctively freeze and lie down on the ground, slow its breathing and heart rate, close its eyes, foam at the mouth, and even produce a terrible smell. This elaborate performance fools its predator into thinking it's already dead, and the opossum can stay like this for hours while waiting for an adversary to lose interest and wander off.

We all face moments in our life when it seems like things just can't get any worse: losing a job, mourning the end of a relationship, being diagnosed with an illness, facing a difficult family situation, or dealing with many mishaps piling up at once. Sometimes we need to just strip our lives down to the bare essentials in order to make it through to the next chapter of our journey. We may find ourselves in solitude, whether we chose it or not, tasked with simply making it to our next day. The opossum reminds us that we don't have to look good or be perfect; we don't have to put on a mask and go to the party and pretend things are okay; we don't have to step into the limelight or be our best self every moment. Sometimes, we survive by doing the minimum we have to do to see it through to the other side. The opossum keeps us company in this deep hermitage, reminding us that playing dead and doing less can be our most inspired adaptive response. We will emerge again, ready to move forward knowing that we have the strength and the power to survive.

Questions to Consider

- When have you faced an existential threat? When moments like that happen, what can you let go of to allow yourself more flexibility and protection?

- Do you give yourself permission to go into healing solitude when you need it, or even a little *before* you need it?

• When things are bad, what tools can you reach for to find a creative and unexpected solution?

Calling the Spirit of the Opossum

If you feel drawn to the lessons of the opossum, you may want to do some journaling or meditating about solitude and stripping away. Hopefully it doesn't happen often, but in a make-or-break time, like those that can come with trauma, grief, or addiction, the opossum can help you reevaluate your priorities and narrow your focus on what it takes to survive. Give yourself permission to not be okay right now. If there is a situation in your life that needs all of your attention, consider what you can let go of for the moment in order to put one foot in front of the other. Time can give us great perspective and offer healing, so do what you need to do to make it to the next day and the next.

A silent retreat is another way to access opossum wisdom. You don't have to devote yourself to a lifetime in a religious order to reap the benefits of time spent alone and in intense reflection, meditation, and prayer. There may be retreat houses or monasteries in your area that offer this kind of short-term hermitage that can provide you with the silent, contemplative downtime you need to move through into a new chapter of your life.

A Prayer for Opossum Energy

Friend opossum, solitary wanderer,
help me find my way through this
dark night of the soul. Help me to
uncover and hold on to only those few
essential things that will see me through
to the other side, so that I may
awaken into a new day and
a new life.

OTTER

Teachings to Remember When Encountering Otters

With their sleek fur, small, dexterous paws, and whiskery mustaches, otters are well loved the world over. Otters live in the sea and in fresh water, in kelp forests and bays, and in rushing rivers. Because of their curiosity, social nature, and humanlike actions such as using tools and holding hands, some indigenous cultures have viewed otters as having strong ties to human beings.

Otters play throughout their lifetime. Young otters will often engage in chasing games, and many otters seem to enjoy sliding and performing acrobatic leaps and tumbles in the water. The otter relies on its curiosity and spends time investigating. Sea otters are among the few animals we know of that use tools, often carrying special rocks with them in a pouch that they use to break open shellfish. They are also the only sea animals who turn over rocks in search of food.

Scientists have found that play provides one of the most powerful platforms for learning and social bonding available to us as humans. Similarly, when otters play, it seems they are helping themselves and each other learn skills they will use in hunting and evading predators. On a storytelling level, otters have a great deal to teach us about the value of play, joy, and even dance.

Otters seem to truly enjoy being otters. Fat or thin, sleek or tousled, in the sea or river, otters seem to relish their ability to swim, dive, and leap. In contrast, we humans often feel overworked and stressed out, never finding time for play or relaxation. A brief vacation once or twice a year can never counterbalance a lifetime of being tied up in our own schedules and worries. The otter reminds us to enjoy the life we've been given. Life is a great gift! Many of us have agile and able bodies with which we can run, jump, leap, swim, and tumble. In fact, any and every person has a body they can enjoy in some way. The otter teaches us that we should always make time to do just this.

Play and relaxation build up our emotional health and our immune systems, releasing the pent-up energy of our busy lives. The otter teaches us that joy is essential.

Questions to Consider

- When was the last time you spent a day, or even an hour, just playing and experiencing joy?

- Can you take five minutes right now to relax, maybe dance, or smile at something beautiful?

- Is there something you've been very rigid about in your life that you can let soften into a more flexible, forgiving approach?

Calling the Spirit of the Otter

If you find yourself stressed out regularly, see if you can spend a couple of minutes looking at how you can put more play into your life. Can you take a five- or ten-minute break and go for a quick walk somewhere delightful? Is there a new restaurant or park you've been wanting to visit? Maybe turn on your favorite music and have a crazy dance break. During the COVID-19 pandemic, when everyone was more or less required to stay at home and most activities were canceled, a friend of mine decided to buy a small inflatable pool for the backyard, where her family could splash and play in a safe environment. These afternoons spent lounging in even a silly inflatable pool were essential in helping my friend get through a really difficult time, and she thanks the spirit of the otter for bringing an essential sense of play to her life.

A Prayer for Otter Energy

Playful otter, sleek and wild,
spinning and dancing in the water,
teach me how to love this life, to dance and sing
and move, even if I look ridiculous. Help me find
the joy that lives in the heart of every moment.

OWL

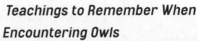

Teachings to Remember When Encountering Owls

The owl flies through the forest, shrouded in darkness and silent as a whisper, always watching. Since ancient Greece, the owl has been seen as a keeper of knowledge, and was messenger and companion to Athena, the goddess of wisdom. With their forward-facing eyes and ability to rotate their necks, we may feel their likeness to us even as we stand in awe of their supernatural perceptive ability. They see what we cannot; they know what is unknown to us.

See Also: Eagle, Hawk, Moth, Vulture

Element: air

- Wise and clear thinking; experienced
- Prudent and deliberative
- Intuitive and lucid

In some cultures, owls are considered unlucky omens of death or emissaries sent by others who wish to do us harm. Some stories contend that they are not birds at all, or even living creatures, but rather ghostly spirits with screeching and otherworldly hoots. But as with all teachings, we get to examine and decide what is meaningful for us. What is an omen, after all? Today we most often think of them as superstitions, but they also speak to a kind of practical knowledge that most of us have turned away from in the modern world.

I'm sure it has happened to you at some point in your life that you got a mysterious "hit" or surge of intuition about a person, a dangerous situation, or an exciting opportunity. There is wisdom in us of which we are not fully conscious. The owl can remind us that by listening to the natural world and to our own intuition, we can open our awareness to the present moment and read a situation quickly and decisively, and then respond with deep intuitive wisdom.

The owl imparts awareness, wisdom, silence, and intuition. The human impulse toward intuitive knowing is itself a way to see in the dark. When the future is murky and we are uncertain which way is best, calling on the spirit of the owl allows us to center ourselves, focus on the present moment, and tap into our inner wisdom and intuitive sense. When we develop these skills, we find we are no longer afraid of the dark, the unseen, the unknowable, the uncertain, even death itself.

In times like these, this is a great gift.

Questions to Consider

- What happens if you move as silently as possible through your day? Can you quiet the internal chatter of your busy mind? How might silent deliberation help you?

- Are you willing to invest time and focus to expand your powers of perception?

- Have you received any intuitive nudges lately that you've been ignoring? Might a "bad" or "unlucky" omen simply be an insight that will keep you safe or alert to a new opportunity?

Calling the Spirit of the Owl

To call the spirit of the owl into your life, work to strengthen your intuitive skills. Often this starts with asking simple yes or no questions and listening to your gut response. For example, on a morning walk you might think to your-self, *Right or left?* and then take a breath and listen for a small voice in your head or a physical tugging in your body one way or the other. Honor the message by following through on the advice to go right or left with an open heart and mind. You may want to keep a page of your daily journal where you note any intuitive impulses, and then return to it with any observations about what was accurate or what you discovered. Often, intuition will lead us down a path we can't justify with our rational mind and to an outcome we don't expect.

A good story about this comes from the education reformer Ken Robinson, who described his frustration with his son's college career. The boy changed majors three times, from economics to Romance languages to art history, and his father felt sure than no good could come from such a chaotic and wide-ranging approach to schooling. The son couldn't account for it either, except to say that it felt right to him. After graduating, he immediately landed in a career he loved, as an art dealer—where he put his knowledge of languages, econom-ics, and art history to use every day.

You may also consider taking up the practice of looking for omens and signs in nature. Tuning in to the natural world opens up a broad landscape of potential intuitive messages. For example, if you have a decision to make and are unsure which direction to move in, find a spot out in the natural world where you feel safe and comfortable, and settle yourself on the ground. Connect to your sur-roundings by taking several deep breaths. Let your thoughts and worries recede from your mind, and call in the spirit of the owl to help you "see in the dark." Then focus on your question or situation . . . and wait. Be patient and recep-tive—sometimes intuitive wisdom is very gentle and can seem insignificant. Perhaps you caught a faint pleasant scent on the wind as you thought of your problem—a flower or a whiff of a campfire. The smell may trigger a memory for you, drawing you back to a time that sheds light on your situation. In turn, this may lead to making a connection that sends you in a creative new direction.

Developing your intuition is a lifelong pursuit that can bring a lot of joy and a renewed sense of connection to the good in the world. Combined with wisdom and common sense, intuitive wisdom is a potent tool.

A Prayer for Owl Energy

Wise owl, one who sees in the dark,
help me to tune in to the living world
that is speaking in every moment.
Open my heart to the wisdom that lives
within me, and help me soar on silent, wise
wings through uncertain times.

PEACOCK

Teachings to Remember When Encountering Peacocks

Peacocks stand out in a crowd in a one-of-a-kind way. *Look at me!* they seem to shout, with the "eyes" of their tail markings seeming to stare right back at you. They strut, dance, and hold sway over their territory in the most gorgeous and extravagant outfit in the animal kingdom. The peacock is an easy symbol of exuberance and splendor and has been a favorite luxurious pet of the elite all over the world for centuries. Peacocks will fiercely defend their territory and have been employed as a defense against cobras or rattlesnakes that might be a danger to livestock or people. In general, humans revere and respect snake-eating birds, which include some species of eagle, hawk, and heron.

See Also: Butterfly, Dragonfly, Hummingbird

Related animals: grouse, heron, pheasant

Elements: earth and air

- Divine
- Splendorous
- Joyful and exuberant

With his loud, shrieking cry, the peacock seems to shout that there may be a time for silence and simplicity, but now is the moment for joy and exuberant celebration. Laughing loudly, showing your work with pride, celebrating the wonder of color, making art and music, dancing and spreading joy—these are the pursuits encouraged by the energy of the peacock. What's more, when we live a life of balance, moments of collective celebration are made all the more profound.

In mythology and culture, the peacock is generally associated with divinity and immorality, and in some Hindu and Buddhist traditions the peacock can break the circle of time, symbolized by the snake. In this way, the peacock invites us not only to consider our own beliefs about the divine and how it moves through the world, but also to look at our relationship with time and death. No one lives forever, a fact that endows our finite lives with meaning and purpose. This is all the more reason to put on our brightest colors and fiercely celebrate life and the present moment in all its variety.

Questions to Consider

- Where do you find the most joy? Can you seek that out today and refresh you sense of beauty and awe?

- When was the last time you pulled out your most beautiful, colorful, or favorite things to wear?

- Are you living life to the fullest? Are you going after what you want?

Calling the Spirit of the Peacock

Peacocks often wander freely around zoos, as well as the grounds of museums or other cultural spaces. The Hollywood Forever cemetery in Los Angeles even hosts a flock. A quick search will likely yield a place you might see them in action, but beware of their territorial nature and give them plenty of space. Even without a peacock in front of you, however, you might take some time to open your senses to the outlandish beauty of the natural world wherever you are—the radiant colors of a sunset, the detailed gradations of a bird's feathers on your porch, or the vibrant green grass after a cleansing rain.

Another way to draw peacock energy to your side is to dress up. Sometimes putting in the effort to polish your shoes, fix your hair, or do whatever it is that makes you feel sharp and attractive can be great medicine. When done in the spirit of joy and celebration, spending time to look your best can help attract your desires. (And maybe the attention of a special someone, too. After all, feeling good in your own skin is the best aphrodisiac.)

A Prayer for Peacock Energy

Enchanting peacock, magnificent and dazzling,
help me to appreciate the beauty of the living world,
and to discern when the time is ripe to let down
my hair, dance with my loved ones, and celebrate
the great moments of life with joy and abandon,
because life is precious, wondrous, and
alive with beauty.

PENGUIN

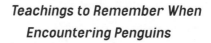

Penguins tend to bring a smile to our face. Dressed in a tuxedo and waddling along with flippers flapping, we just love their silly, sweet looks and behavior. Authors and artists have created all sorts of stories featuring penguins, including a documentary that follows the touching true story of an emperor penguin family living in the unforgiving Antarctic. These social animals are also relatively fearless when it comes to human beings, making them seem less wild than some of their animal counterparts. This might be because penguins have no predators on land—sea animals such as seals and orcas hunt them in the water—but we read their behavior as friendly, amiable, with a sense of fearless curiosity. Penguins sometimes make me think of Charlie Chaplin's classic character of the Tramp, who moves through the world with naive bravery and an openhearted trust of others. It's certainly appealing to think of living in a benevolent world with this kind of openness and simplicity.

See also: Seal, Seagull

Related animals: dodo bird, sea lion, walrus

Elements: water and earth

- Masterful
- Fearless
- Happy

Penguins spend half of their life in the water, and many generations ago their wings adapted to flippers. Whatever gawkiness they have on land they make up for in the water, where they dive, spin, and arc as though they are flying through the air.

You may have experienced a time when a steep learning curve made you feel like a penguin on land. Learning a new job, a new skill, or a foreign language or navigating the layout of an unfamiliar city may have made you think you would never be able to adapt. For example, you probably don't remember it now, but learning to drive a car can be like this. The brain gets overloaded as it juggles practicing hand-eye coordination, keeping rules, limits, and regulations straight, and even making life-and-death decisions on the fly. Yet within a pretty short time, driving becomes second nature—so much so that you might arrive home from work and have little to no memory of how you navigated there safely. Your instinctive brain has taken over.

Whenever I feel overwhelmed by the clumsy discomfort of learning something new, I call out to the penguin. In the spirit of this bird, I can remember that being awkward is okay and that adapting to new elements and swimming in new waters can and will become second nature with enough time and practice. The penguin teaches me that I too can learn to "fly in the water" in ways I previously thought impossible.

Questions to Consider

- Have you been overwhelmed with learning a new skill? Can you enjoy your initial clumsiness as if you were a cute penguin on land?

- Are you adapting to new ideas and new situations with grace?

- Have you been wary of others lately? Is now a good time to extend a friendly smile or introduce yourself to someone new?

Calling the Spirit of the Penguin

Acquiring and mastering a new skill takes practice, determination, and the ability to adapt. The penguin has adapted to two different elements and can provide inspiration and encouragement for any new pursuit you might want to begin. Even if you are not in the position to tackle a new project or a new job, consider picking up a skill or form of creative expression you've always wanted to learn. We're wired to seek out comfort, so it's easy to avoid learning or trying new things. We might disrupt our routines, look ridiculous, or fail completely, but approaching new ideas and skills with the friendly fearlessness of the penguin can be a great way to broaden your horizons. Furthermore, growing in this way creates new pathways in the brain, keeping it supple and engaged throughout your lifetime. Finally, building knowledge has an exponential quality. That is, learning almost anything will inevitably increase your abilities in other areas of your life as well. If you're comfortable drawing, for example, trying to sculpt might feel intimidating, but practicing in three dimensions can help advance your skills at two-dimensional art. I have heard many people say they finally understood the grammar of their own language only through studying another one. Countless professional athletes have upped their game by practicing ballet. Let the penguin be your guide in learning to swim in new waters with instinctive poise.

A Prayer for Penguin Energy

Friend penguin, who swims with such grace
it seems that you fly through the sea,
help me to reach out to new ideas and
new skills with a friendly, curious nature,
teach me how to become a fearless navigator
in the course of my life's work.

PIG

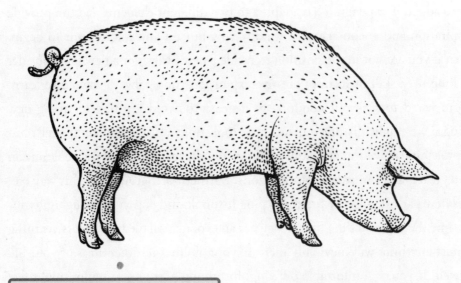

Related animals: boar, javelina, wild pig

Element: earth

- Friendly
- Abundant
- Free

Teachings to Remember When Encountering Pigs

Pigs seem to have a confusing reputation. On one hand, the word connotes someone who is dirty, messy, greedy, slovenly, or rude. On the other hand, we know that pigs are highly intelligent, social, and friendly animals. Many people consider them just as wonderful as dogs or cats. Pigs do like to wallow in mud, as they don't sweat and it cools their skin—and they don't seem to care if it's socially acceptable or not. This is big pig medicine: doing what feels good and enjoying it thoroughly.

A happy pig radiates contentment and enjoyment of life, relishing the pure loveliness of being alive in a physical body, right here and right now. Enjoying the moment is one of the greatest lessons of the natural world, and animals in particular. Because pigs are emotional creatures and form close bonds with others just as we do, it's easy to see them as a model for us of this powerful teaching. When a pig is happily lazing about in the sunlight, you can see and feel the gentle, restful bliss of the present moment as it expresses in their body and on their face. Staying in the present moment has always been a struggle for human, even after thousands of years of spiritual and philosophical teaching.

We live in the present moment. There's no escaping it; our bodies live here and now only. Yet our storytelling mind busily spins yarns about the past (memory and regret) and the future (fantasy and anxiety) in ways that are both an incredible gift and a terrible curse. It's a gift in that with this amazing power to time travel in our minds, we can dream up incredible works of architecture, storytelling, and art over the centuries. We can build on the knowledge of others long gone. The curse of course is that unless we can see that the mind is just telling stories, we become attached to the stories as if they were reality, and this causes suffering. The mind then gets addicted to suffering and perpetuates a cycle of avoiding the present and believing faulty agreements and stories.

Pigs teach us to enjoy the present moment, especially when life is good. Anxiety and regret rob us of the joy of the present. For example, someone with a severe anxiety disorder can lose hold of a good moment in an instant by having an anxious thought about what could happen in the future or what's happened in the past. A beautiful sunny day turns into a panic about sunburn and skin cancer, or a gift from a loved one turns into crippling regret over forgetting a family member's birthday four years ago. Pigs can be a powerful ally for those who are learning to retrain their thinking and behavior into more freedom and joy in the moment.

Pigs are also associated with gluttony, of course, but this too is an unhelpful story. We are all allowed to enjoy the moment and be grateful for we have. In fact, joy is an appropriate way to celebrate good news and abundance and keeps us grounded in what nourishes and sustains us.

Questions to Consider

- Have you been dwelling too much in the past . . . or in the future? What can you do right now to ground yourself in the present moment?

- What do you most enjoy about your day-to-day life?

- What happens when you start from a place of friendliness to those you meet out in the world?

- Do you give thanks when you feel satiated, or do you feel guilty or worried?

Calling the Spirit of the Pig

Human beings enjoy good food, and a great way to connect with the teachings the pig offers regarding the present moment and abundance is to create and share a wonderful meal with others.

This meal can be anything you like. As you put together your feast, you might consider what foods would most fill you with appreciation for the abundance of planet earth. If you have time and energy, make your meal from scratch using foods that start in a form as close to their source as possible. Whatever time and energy you put into the creation of your meal will imbue it with significance.

The smell of freshly baked bread brings us right into the present moment. Fresh vegetables, fruits, and grains all speak to the richness of the earth, as does fresh cold water. If the weather is good, an outdoor feast on a blanket or at a picnic table can be delightful. Spending time preparing food and eating with loved ones nourishes body and soul.

Before, during, or after your meal, you may want to pause in gratitude not only for the food you are eating but for the planet that provides it and the people who prepared it. After your wonderful meal, you may want to spend some time simply being—perhaps sitting in the sun, utterly content in the present moment.

A Prayer for Pig Energy

Sweet pig, who shows the way to
contentedness and abundance in your
friendly, joyful being, help me to
live and be grateful for this present moment.
Teach me how to appreciate the bounty of
the great Mother Earth.

RABBIT

See also: Coyote, Crow, Fox, Spider

Related animals: hare, jackrabbit, mouse, pika, rat

Element: earth

- Clever
- Fertile
- Discreet

Teachings to Remember When Encountering Rabbits

Female rabbits can give birth to litters five times a year, making them one of the most fertile mammals on earth and accounting for their presence all over the world. Being so widespread may be why rabbit teachings share significant similarities in many cultures. They are wily tricksters as well as keepers of immortality, sexual joy, and fruitfulness, and they have a special relationship with the moon. In Japan, a rabbit who lives on the moon makes lunar-shaped cakes called mochi. The moon and the rabbit both reflect the cyclical nature of time, fertility, and the kind of unending renewal that connotes immortality.

In many Native American stories, the rabbit is a trickster like the raven, coyote, and spider, but it is the only prey animal with that distinction. The rabbit's specialty as a small animal is turning the tables and outwitting larger predators such as the lynx, otter, and mountain lion. However, the rabbit does not always win in these matchups, and sometimes gets humiliated or even eaten. Luckily, there are always more rabbits being born. Other stories, like those of Peter Rabbit and Br'er Rabbit, play up this trickster capacity in a gentler context with sweet, furry, dancing characters who get into and out of mostly harmless scrapes.

The rabbit has mastered hiding in plain sight. Its dusky coloring, ears that fold back into a low profile, and ability to freeze on a dime make it almost impossible to see until it takes off in great, zigzagging leaps. The silent, soft footsteps of the rabbit share the lesson of treading gently for our own safety and also in reverence of the natural world.

The rabbit's fertility energy can certainly be called upon by those looking to expand their family, but also for subtler aspects of fruitfulness. Rabbits remind us that creativity and productivity operate best in cycles, just as the moon waxes and wanes, transforming from an empty sliver into a ripe, full circle on a monthly basis. If you're looking for abundance that mirrors the population growth of the rabbit, one of the best things you can do is to add rest and recovery to your sprints of hard work, learning new things, or pushing your limits. In this way, you come into the natural, helpful rhythm of the rabbit, who knows all about exponential results.

Questions to Consider

- Have you felt too small or timid to take on a big problem or face down an obstacle in your path? What if you had the wily charms of the rabbit and could turn the tables to your advantage?

- What practices do you have in place to honor your own natural cycles, whether physical, emotional, or energetic?

- What could you bring to fruition in the spirit of the fertile rabbit this week?

Calling the Spirit of the Rabbit

If you ever think of compounding interest, it's probably in a financial or economic context. Yet compounding exists in all kinds of natural processes as well. Think of an avalanche that starts with just a little bit of movement and gathers power and force until it becomes a huge wall of destruction. The health of a tree is a sweeter, slower example—with each passing year it gets wider and stronger, growing a deeper root system and gaining the resources to put more leaves out into the air, which can in turn catch more sun and feed even more efficient growth. As a species, rabbits in any given habitat can establish themselves in the same way—with one pair quickly becoming hundreds.

Consider adding a rabbit talisman to your altar if you're trying to expand your family, start a new business venture, or begin an educational program or if you want to invite general abundance and productivity into your life. Rabbits can remind you that big results compound through small actions, repeated over time. An image or stone sculpture of a bunny can remind you to enjoy the journey, know when to let loose and when to step back, and never forget that everything happens in cycles and seasons.

A Prayer for Rabbit Energy

Mother rabbit, hopping in the shadow
of the moon, let me follow in your gentle
footsteps, at times unseen, at times dancing.
I promise to keep my eyes open for abundance
as all things wax and wane.

RACCOON

See also: Bear, Squirrel, Skunk

Related animals: mouse, pigeon, rat

Element: earth

- Resourceful and adaptable
- Mischievous
- Balanced

Teachings to Remember When Encountering Raccoons

Have you ever been asleep and woken to a loud crash outside? You might not see them in the moment, but raccoons, with their little bandit faces, may be responsible for the nighttime shenanigans. Playful problem-solvers, raccoons can get into all sorts of trouble from our perspective. But from their point of view, they have every right to adapt and live alongside us—after all, we surround our homes with tons of good stuff to eat, play with, and use for nests. Along with pigeons, rats, and squirrels, raccoons have proven to be incredibly resourceful in changing their wild habits and behaviors to suit a wide range of environments. Unlike their wilder cousins, they are able to survive where others animal might not. This is a powerful teaching not to be overlooked. We human beings must work to heal Mother Earth by restoring natural habitats and maintaining wild spaces, and at the same time we can admire the animals that persist by being resourceful in new circumstances.

In folklore, raccoons portend mischief. Getting into trash cans, helping themselves inside pet doors, and terrorizing chicken coops all underscore this reputation. Their capable hands and high intelligence allow them to figure out how to unlock and investigate all kinds of places humans would rather they leave alone, as well as pick up and carry away items like pet bowls and even small area rugs.

Alongside this reputation for chaos and mischief, however, raccoons are also known for their habit of dipping food into water before eating it. This habit has been observed by so many different cultures that many words for raccoon in other languages translate into something akin to "washing-bear." While it's not clear whether raccoons are washing their food or not, the folkloric association with washing and cleaning is still very strong. In this way, the raccoon embodies not only the symbolic aspects of chaos, but also those of order and cleanliness.

Questions to Consider

- What bounty can you find around you? When things get tough, can thinking fast on your feet and adapting to changing circumstances help you find treasure in what might look like trash?

- What we think of as mischief is often just someone coming from a different perspective. If you are frustrated by a "raccoon" in your life, perhaps a toddler spreading chaos, can you take a moment and try to see the world through their eyes?

- Sometimes absolute order is not all it's cracked up to be. How can you introduce some positive, rejuvenating change into your day to shake things up and make things fresh and fun?

Calling the Spirit of the Raccoon

It's always interesting to observe a raccoon as it investigates, thinks, and figures its way toward its next meal. There are many safe ways to do this, including heaps of entertaining videos of raccoon hijinks.

Consider the teachings of the raccoon and how they might inform your life. How do you react to change? If a situation feels less than ideal, but is utterly out of your control, can you find some new ways to adapt? Sometimes it's important to resist change, but it can also be a great gift to accept some situations as they are and move forward.

A Prayer for Raccoon Energy

Mischief-maker, balancing chaos and order,
little washing-bear, friend raccoon,
teach me how to accept and adapt to
new information and new situations. Help me
learn how to unlock my own playful wisdom.

RATTLESNAKE

Teachings to Remember When Encountering Rattlesnakes

Snakes are powerful teachers, and when we approach them with respect, they have much to show us. All thirty-six species of rattlesnakes are native to the Americas, and the rattlesnake plays an important role in the ancient mythologies of Mexico, notably in the embodiment of the half bird and half rattlesnake Quetzalcoatl, creator of the world and humankind.

The rattlesnake inspires fear of its venomous bite. Yet they usually only bite if provoked, and if treated quickly, their bites are rarely fatal. They also have a built-in alarm: when they feel threatened or their space is being invaded, they give fair warning by shaking their rattle. If you've ever heard it in person, you know this sound stops you in your tracks and brings you right into the present moment. Interestingly, rattlesnakes are not born with their rattles—they build them through the shedding process over the course of their lives.

The rattlesnake is associated with the element of fire, partly because they need outside heat sources like the sun or a warm rock to regulate their body temperature. They also represent the fiery power of the unquenchable spirit. By connecting with the rattlesnake, you can learn to create boundaries and focus your fiery emotions in a productive and fruitful way. For example, anger can give you the energy to leave a dangerous situation or relationship and energize causes of justice and fairness, but it can also be toxic. Often, anger masks more vulnerable emotions like hurt or fear. The rattlesnake teaches us how to balance our temper by moving away from situations that may make us "overheated" and to find life-giving sources of energy and bask in them, storing up good reserves for future use. Snake medicine brings vitality, stamina, and respect for the life force in all of us.

Questions to Consider

- When is the last time that your temper got the better of you? What actions could you take now to help modulate your venom?

- Are your boundaries giving you space to feel safe and protected? Can you build trust in yourself by saying no and yes only when you really mean it?

- When was the last time you spent some time in the sun, just being?

Calling the Spirit of the Rattlesnake

You don't need to get cozy with a rattlesnake in order to learn its wisdom! Respect the rattlesnake's boundaries and it will respect yours. There are natural history museums and zoos that may have live rattlesnakes or replicas, which can be a safe way to enjoy their presence.

You might also consider making your own rattle to place on your altar and use in ceremony whenever you want to remind yourself of the rattlesnake's wise teachings. Rattles can be made out of empty gourds or even old containers filled with dried beans.

A Prayer for Rattlensake Energy

Honored one, weaving in and out
of the sunlight, help me in finding balance.
With your guidance, I know how to say,
"This is my limit" and to use judgment and
to honor anger as a force for change.
Rattlesnake, honored one,
I seek your wisdom.

SALMON

Related animals: clown fish, minnow, rainbow trout, sardine, sunfish, swordfish, tuna

Element: water

- Knowledgeable and wise
- Determined
- Creative

Teachings to Remember When Encountering Salmon

For the ancient Celts of Ireland and Wales, the salmon is a symbol of wisdom and knowledge. In Welsh mythology the salmon of Llyn Llyw is the oldest animal in Britain, and in one Irish story the Salmon of Knowledge became wise by eating nine hazelnuts that fell into the Well of Wisdom. Salmon is also sacred to the people of the Pacific Northwest, where it is a powerful symbol of life.

Salmon are born in fresh water, often in streams far from the sea, and make their way to the wide ocean to spend most of their adult lives. When they are ready, they return to fresh water to spawn, often to the exact same place they were hatched. They carry the memory of place for their whole lives and navigate back to it by instinct. This remarkable journey takes perseverance, and the salmon must overcome many hazards along the way. Once they have completed this cycle, the salmon die in the stream where they were born—their bodies feeding the surrounding ecosystem and in turn their young, just as true knowledge nourishes future generations.

Salmon belong to the great family of fish of all sizes and temperaments that live in salt and freshwater all over the earth. They range from solitary creatures to members of massive schools that move in perfect synchrony. Consider how the attributes of these various fast-moving and glittering creatures of water, their balance and ease, might inform your healing journey—especially when it comes to your emotional life. Are you on a lifelong emotional journey, like the salmon, or do you prefer to stay in the dark depths of the ocean? Do you leap into the air or dart along the surface? Remember, none of these is right or wrong; this is simply the bounty of fish medicine in its many forms.

As creatures of water, fish are also associated with emotions and the healthy flow of a balanced emotional life. The salmon might be thought to be the bearer of emotional wisdom. Salmon medicine reminds us to honor our emotional beginnings and to make life's journey with awareness of our feelings and how they manifest in our actions, desires, and relationships. The circumstances around us will be as changeable as water, but we get to chart our course home to our truest self. This is the seat of your creative power, and you have an unfailing compass that will guide you there—you only have to follow it.

Questions to Consider

- What does wisdom mean to you? Who is the wisest person you know? How do you share your knowledge with others?

- Take a moment to check in with yourself: Are you holding any tension that needs to be addressed? Are there blocks in your emotional flow?

- Where is your creative center, your home? It might be a physical location, an activity that brings you joy, or an authentic relationship that enlivens you. What is your earliest memory of this place? How can you come home to this place more often?

Calling the Spirit of the Salmon

If you live in an area where you can safely observe wild salmon or local wild fish in a river or even an ocean setting, that is a wonderful gift. If not, you can still connect to the spirit of this silvery being of inspiration by spending time near a river or other body of water. One practice is to ask salmon to help you answer a particular question or give you guidance about a situation.

At the water's edge, still your mind, and let your emotions and any difficult mental "knots" from the day ease, loosen, and flow. In your mind's eye, imagine a deep pool in the heart of a forest, fed by a clear underground source, its surface dappled with sunlight and shade from the surrounding trees. You notice a large silver salmon swimming in the pool; this is the Salmon of Knowledge, and if you ask your question and wait with patience and peace in your heart, you might hear your answer whispered to you from the depths.

A Prayer for Salmon Energy

I am the rushing of the river.
I am a deep pool in a dark forest.
I am a silver arrow in the open sea.
Wisdom keeper, sister salmon,
unlock my mind and open the door to wisdom.

SEAGULL

Teachings to Remember When Encountering Seagulls

Do you remember the first time you saw the ocean? Maybe you grew up nearby, in which case the memory may be so early that it seems like a part of your consciousness itself. If not, that moment probably activated your soul and opened your heart. The vast expanse of water and sky; the roiling or gentle surf; the distant, limitless horizon. The sea is simply breathtaking. All life originated in the sea, and I sometimes think we can feel its stirrings at a molecular level.

Seabirds have a special place in ocean life—dipping into the water, poking through the sand on the shore, soaring on its gusts of wind—and never leaving its side.

Seagulls are living symbols of this coastal life. Their iconic, piercing cry brings the sea immediately to mind. They can be a nuisance to some; like raccoons and other resourceful animals, seagulls will eat just about anything and have adapted to life alongside human beings quite well. As social creatures, they flock in great, noisy numbers, with no regard for human decorum. They'll

See also: Penguin, Seal

Related animals: albatross, auk, cormorant, gannet, kingfisher, pelican, sea duck, skimmer, tern

Elements: air, water, and earth

- Inquisitive and resourceful
- Flexible
- Determined

tear apart a beachgoer's picnic basket and even steal food right out of your hands! Seagulls are generalists when it comes to food, and this is part of their animal wisdom. They don't rely on any one kind of food or even any one way of getting it. They're the only animal, for example, that will drop clams and mussels onto hard surfaces from above to open them. Creative, smart, and resourceful—we can learn plenty from the seagull.

Seagulls have what you might call a "diversified portfolio" of options available to them when it comes to food, nesting, and places to hang out. They're equally comfortable bobbing in the waves, foraging on dry land, or soaring above it all. They keep their options open, and their ingenuity is impressive. A lot of messages in the world tell us there's one "right" way to do things, dictating how we get an education, how we make a living, where we should live, how much stuff we need to buy . . . and the list goes on.

There are so many ways to be a parent, an artist, a student, a partner, a worker, a seeker. You get to choose what's right for you, and the seagull can remind you that you have only scratched the surface of the available options. With the seagull's key lessons of determination and resourcefulness, so much is possible through such a wide variety of tactics. Whenever we are faced with a situation in which we need to try more options, keep moving forward despite setbacks, or be willing to annoy others in pursuit of our goals, the spirit of the seagull can help.

Questions to Consider

- Is there a project or situation you're about to give up on? How can you apply a renewed sense of determination and resourcefulness to see it through?

- Are there options you've been ignoring that may warrant a closer look, even if they seemed far-fetched at first?

Calling the Spirit of the Seagull

When you combine determination and resourcefulness you get the seagull's mantra: there's always an option. Whenever you feel backed into a corner or trapped by a circumstance in your life, call on the spirit of the seagull to help you come up with creative options.

One way to do this is by using your personal journal. First, make sure you're in a comfortable, safe space, and take a few deep breaths as you settle into the present moment. Then take a few minutes to consider the issue you want to concentrate on, and start to list the different ways you could approach it. Be as creative as you can, and remember that these don't have to be concrete, plausible alternatives; the point of this is to remind yourself that you have agency, creativity, and freedom within you at all times. So if one of the items on your list is "run away and join the circus" and that seems just a bit unlikely, that's fine. You're simply practicing stretching those wings and breathing possibility back into your life.

Pulling ourselves out of a story in which we feel trapped can be difficult, so this exercise can sometimes feel like pushing a boulder uphill. Whenever you feel stuck, it may help to close your eyes and imagine you're standing on a long stretch of open coast all by yourself, with the enormous, peaceful, expansive sea in front of you. Feel the wind in your face, and spend a few moments watching as high above you the wheeling seagulls dart and spin through the open air, full of confidence and ready to swoop in on the next opportunity.

A Prayer for Seagull Energy

Canny and able, friend seagull, be
my guide as I learn how to unlock
the stories that keep me from seeing
that the world is as full of possibility,
as rife with plot twists and alternative endings,
as the sea is endless and full of fish.

SEAL

See also: Dolphin, Otter, Penguin

Related animals: elephant seal, sea lion, walrus

Element: water

- Friendly
- Creative
- Graceful

Teachings to Remember When Encountering Seals

Seals have captivated the cultural imagination of those who live by and on the sea for ages. The Inuit honor a goddess named Sedna who appears in the form of a seal and is a creatrix and benevolent mother goddess. The Celts still tell stories about the selkie, a group of mythological shapeshifting women who shed their sealskins to dance on the shores of the sea by moonlight. Humans are drawn to these playful, sleek, and graceful animals with the dark and mysterious eyes. Seals also seem to have a natural friendliness with human beings, and when seen in the distance in the water, it's very possible to understand how they might be mistaken for human beings themselves. The human capacity for wonder and imagination brings these special seal stories to life.

Water is the realm of emotion and deep imagination. Myth, symbol, archetypes, poetry, and art all rise up from its swirling depths. Hand in hand with the gift of imagination is the gift of wonder. Children tend to have easy access to this realm, diving into immersive make-believe or relishing the fear of a spooky story or the alluring surprise of a strange creature. As adults, we sometimes forget that we have nothing to lose and everything to gain when we set our bias for rationality aside and cultivate our sense of wonder and our amazing imaginative capacity. Wonder and imagination tend to manifest as the creative expression that so many of us seek, after all.

In order to truly dive deep into the vast seas of imagination, it helps to have a playful mindset. Even though it can sometimes be dangerous or disorienting, life can also be *fun*. The seal nudges us awake with its wet, whiskered nose, reminding us to explore, relish, and enjoy any chance we get to dive into the emotional, symbol-rich, and wonder-filled environment of the imagination.

Questions to Consider

- When was the last time you felt a sense of wonder and awe? Is this something you can make a point to cultivate today?

- What fantastic, out-there stories did you love as a child that you might reread today?

- Have you been bogged down in too much work and a sense of duty? The next time you feel overwhelmed, can you give in to the world's request that you take some time to relax and play?

Calling the Spirit of the Seal

You may think you have no imagination or that you're not a creative person, but it's far more likely that you've simply repressed these natural human instincts over time. Our culture tells us to "stop daydreaming" or "be practical," and eventually we adopt these imperatives as necessary truths, stifling our creativity and sense of wonder. The good news is that imagination waits just outside our normal routine, ready for us to reclaim it at any moment with play and exploration.

A great way to revive your imagination muscles is by practicing the simple art of daydreaming. You may wish to begin this exercise with a small ritual in which you call the spirit of the playful seal to help you. Daydreaming is easy and can of course be done anywhere and anytime, but in order to counterbalance the cultural expectations that may tell you that you are "wasting time," it can be helpful to carve out some special time just for this. You can call this your woolgathering time.

You can start with some fun prompts like imagining what it might be like to be the size of a mouse or a mountain. You could also try to put your mind in the body of one of your power animals to see what insights may be gained that way. Swim with the seals, fly with the eagle, or go for a walk in the savanna with a pride of lions or a herd of elephants . . . the possibilities are endless.

A Prayer for Seal Energy

Friend seal, playful and bright,
help me recapture my sense of wonder,
play, and imagination. Teach me how to
glide through the sometimes troubled waters
of my emotional self with grace.

SHARK

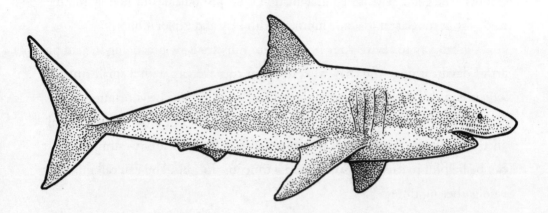

Teachings to Remember When Encountering Sharks

Sharks, the great hunters of the sea, slice through open water always moving forward, with keen senses attuned to everything around them. Like the snake, the shark holds primordial fear and fascination for humans, along with a heap of domesticated ideas and stories thanks to things like *Jaws* and Shark Week. In reality, thousands of different species of sharks, from the enormous and docile whale shark down to the tiny dwarf lantern shark, make up an essential, life-giving part of all ocean ecosystems. Contrary to our stories, there are no villains or heroes in the natural world—we all have a special, sacred place in the web of life.

We can think of shark energy in terms of relentless focus, expanded range of sensory experience, grace, and mastery of the water—the element tied to emotion on the medicine wheel. Some of our fear of sharks can also be traced to this elemental aspect. Our emotional world can feel "below the surface," full of danger we can't see and moved by currents over which we have little control. In this way, getting comfortable with shark medicine brings us into alignment with the great oceanic force of our own emotional life. If we spend all our time skimming across the surface, we do make ourselves vulnerable to emotional sneak attacks. Long buried or unprocessed emotions can torpedo us out of our comfort zone and do serious damage. But if we dive below and meet what's really going on for us with a courageous heart, we can learn to be as at home with our emotions as a shark is in deep water.

Indigenous island cultures have long honored sharks for their strength and power, which is almost never directed at killing and eating human beings. In fact, we are far more deadly to sharks than they are to us. This is another way that sharks can teach us about emotion. Big feelings like grief or rage sometimes feel dangerous, even life-threatening, until we realize that we can feel anything safely by letting it flow through us without acting on it. Our fear of feelings, like our fear of sharks, bears little relationship to the actual threat they pose to us.

Sharks are known for their grace and speed, cutting through the sea at an average speed of five miles an hour. Some sharks, including the iconic great white, can swim in shockingly fast sprints to avoid danger or close in on prey. You might want to call on the shark when your energy is flagging to help muster that burst of creative energy that will carry you over the finish line.

Sharks also have expanded senses beyond sight, hearing, smell, taste, and touch that allow them to sense electrical fields, pressure changes, even the tiniest movements in the water. Some sharks must keep swimming without rest so that they can pump oxygenated water through their gills, and most sharks can't swim backward due to the shape of their pectoral fins. There is a useful metaphorical teaching in this. We often get stuck in our past, ruminating on regrets and past hurts in a way that can stop our progress toward the next stage in our lives. When this happens, we can allow the teachings of the shark to lead us forward, always forward into new waters and kinder seas.

- Have you been allowing an issue or situation to hold you back? Can you imagine yourself as a shark, keen senses feeling your way forward with intent and purpose?

- What areas of your life could benefit from moving swiftly through them with the cutting grace of a shark?

- Are you comfortable diving into the depths of your emotional life, knowing you are safe and welcome there even when it may feel dangerous or difficult?

Calling the Spirit of the Shark

Have you ever considered swimming with sharks? You certainly don't have to in order to connect with the spirit of the shark, but even imagining this activity can inspire awe and reverence for shark medicine. Going to the ocean in person is another way to come closer to the enormous, deep, and mysterious power it holds. As you spend time near the sea, or near any body of water, you can easily cast your imagination out into the great wide depths to call on this powerful animal and its teachings.

Here is a short meditation to call the spirit of the shark into your life. Find a safe and comfortable place to sit. Take three deep breaths and allow your muscles to relax as you imagine yourself hovering over the vast ocean with no land in sight. The day is bright and sunny, and the water below you crisp and blue. Now, dive down into the depths. Look around you, feeling into all your senses as you imagine them coming alive under the water. Next, if it feels right, imagine you see or sense a shimmering ball in front of you—a manifestation of a particular goal or dream you have. Feel the amazing speed and skill of the shark welling up in you and push forward, gliding effortlessly through the water toward your goal. Take a few moments to breathe in your accomplishment. To gently close the meditation, rise to the surface of the water. You may want to write down in your journal any insights or images that came to you.

A Prayer for Shark Energy

Shark spirit, great hunter in the deep sea, help me to move effortlessly and swiftly toward my goal. Help me cut through all obstacles in front of me. May inspiration rocket through my being and propel me toward my dreams.

SHEEP

Teachings to Remember When Encountering Sheep

Calling someone a "sheep" as an insult reflects a profound ignorance about creatures who live and thrive in herds. It underestimates the mutual aid and protection of a herd, its nurturing social bonds, and the wisdom of many minds and bodies working together. From a human perspective, it may not feel comfortable to think of only ever existing in a cohesive group, but for sheep and other creatures being alone is far more terrifying. I have a friend with a solitary goat which has grown attached to her flock of chickens, creating his own sense of a "herd" that keeps him calm and connected.

> **See Also:** Cow, Goat
>
> **Related animals:** antelope, bighorn sheep, mountain goat, wildebeest
>
> **Element:** earth
>
> • Compassionate and gentle
> • Flexible
> • Deferential

Sheep have a long history in religious and cultural tradition for representing peace, compassion, and gentleness, all qualities that can be cultivated while also maintaining one's sense of individuality and thoughtfulness. At the same time, rams (male sheep), notably the bighorn sheep, which are native to North America, convey power and strength. These magnificent creatures climb high into the mountains to avoid predators, sure-footed where other animals or humans would falter. All this serves as a reminder that the prevalent stories about certain animals and their teachings or powers may not be true for you and there is always more to discover in the complexity and variety of the natural world.

Domestic sheep raised for their wool are usually sheared seasonally. If we look closely at our lives and pay attention to the cycles that come and go in them, we can see that we too may experience regular times of building up and times of letting go. Some spiritual traditions associate these cycles with the moon or the tides, which have their own regular cycles of waning and waxing. By reflecting on this common pattern we can acknowledge the ebb and flow with grace and equanimity, knowing that everything works in cycles and the current situation, whether positive or negative, will always pass.

It's worth taking a deeper look at the sheep's reputation for following. People have kept flocks of sheep for centuries, and the archetype of the shepherd provides an important cultural touchstone. Christianity, Judaism, and Islam all rely on the metaphorical relationship between the flock and the shepherd as a model for spiritual leadership, and this has become part of our collective imagination. I think it's interesting that wild herds of sheep get along fine without a human leader. Domestic herds can do well on their own too, and often a shepherd is there to maintain ownership, not to guide the flock. The old story of sheep being ignorant followers has long been employed to justify leaders who prize authority and power over gentler qualities of listening, restoring balance, and supporting well-being. True authority in this context comes from the shepherd's ability to care for and serve those in her or his charge and from the reciprocal, collaborative relationship between species. In the midst of a calm and happy herd, wandering through pastures and munching grass, it's impossible not to feel connected to the earth and the wisdom of all her sacred creatures. No matter how you feel about flocks and shepherds, I encourage you to trust your own wisdom and courageously lead and follow according to careful discernment—for both are essential.

Questions to Consider

- Are you being asked to let go of something that you've been holding on to for too long?

- Are you being called to a peacemaking position? Is there a conflict in your life that could benefit from gentle, peace-oriented leadership?

Calling the Spirit of the Sheep

To connect with the gentle peace and wisdom of a herd of sheep, you may want to reflect, journal, and meditate on your own beliefs about authority, leadership, and whom you choose to follow in your life. Who have been your mentors and guides? Are there changes you can make to align your life more with the values they represent? If you determine that a figure or mentor you used to find influential no longer fits your worldview, consider how to gently release their influence in your life, perhaps through a ritual of letting go where you visualize thanking them for all they have done for you in the past but acknowledge that it is time for you to move forward.

A Prayer for Sheep Energy

Peaceful friend sheep, woolly follower,
help me to discern true, authentic authority
in the world; teach me to be gentle, to
choose compassion, and to follow
only in the footsteps of those worthy
of my trust.

SKUNK

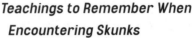

Teachings to Remember When Encountering Skunks

Imagine having a cute face, a distinctive black-and-white outfit, and a reputation for being great at pest control, but everyone only knows you for one thing: your stinky defensive maneuver. Once you know, you know. The smell sticks around for a long time, the skunk knows how to aim with precision, and its stench can be so strong and irritating that it can cause temporary blindness. A tiny skunk can scare off someone as big as a bear. In turns out that being famous for your stink actually buys you a lot of peace and quiet in the natural world, though. Predators stay away, and the skunk rarely has to engage in any kind of conflict.

Knowledge about the animal world thankfully no longer blindly claims that nature is "red in tooth and claw," as the poet Alfred, Lord Tennyson, once said. The truth is

See also: Ant, Rattlesnake

Related animals: bombardier beetle, boxer crab, hornet, Malaysian exploding ant, pistol shrimp, porcupine, Texas horned lizard

Element: earth

• Peaceful
• Curious
• Respected

far more nuanced and complex, a world of community, of give-and-take, of the ebbs and flows of starvation and excess. The skunk is a living embodiment of this change. It does not run or hide from a fight, but it builds a reputation that keeps it safe through its pungent warning. When it is attacked, it's often only by a young and inexperienced animal who quickly learns their lesson. The skunk is a literal teacher, outlining its boundaries with utter clarity.

It may feel necessary to fight back in order to defend ourselves; there are so many opportunities in our world to choose violence. Humans have the tools and the means to wreak unimaginable violence on others, and we arm ourselves to the teeth in the name of "personal safety" in the face of perceived threats. And yet there are so many alternatives. We can set strong boundaries, make our power clear in no uncertain terms, address real threats instead of imagined ones, and earn respect through a reputation for nonviolence. Like the skunk, our nonviolence can have unmistakable and memorable power and strength.

Questions to Consider

- Are you in the midst of a challenging situation that could use an alternative approach?

- Is there a situation in your life that would benefit from a nonviolent, creative solution?

Calling the Spirit of the Skunk

The skunk is an apt symbol for creative self-defense, and many martial arts disciplines teach that violence must be a very last resort. To call on the powerful teachings of the skunk, consider learning or practicing one of these methods of self-defense or training in nonviolent conflict mediation and resolution. In a world that can feel violent and assaultive, and in a culture of fear, we can forget how many tools we really have at our disposal to deal with threats and conflicts. Working with these disciplines and methods boosts our inner confidence, which inevitably radiates out into our physical being. In turn, not unlike the distinctive markings of the skunk, the resulting poise and composure you project will tell all those around you that you are not to be messed with, even as you are committed to a nonviolent worldview.

A Prayer for Skunk Energy

Friend skunk, one who knows
how to hold nonviolence and strength
together tightly in the heart; teach me
how to create meaningful boundaries,
to show others in my walk and in my speech,
that I believe in peace,
while holding the power to defend myself
in times of struggle.

SLOTH

Teachings to Remember When Encountering Sloths

Sloths are everywhere at the moment. I don't mean on the streets of your city, of course, but they're everywhere in the popular imagination. When an animal who has been around the planet for millennia captures the attention of so many, it's fun to ask ourselves why. In what ways are we desperate for the particular medicine of the sloth? My guess is that we are drawn to the sloth as a counterpoint for our current moment.

See Also: Turtle

Related animals: anteater, armadillo, koala, snail

Element: earth

- Restful
- Peaceful
- Unassuming

Where we are frenzied and chaotic, the sloth is slow and deliberate. Where we are desperate to stand out and be on display, the sloth settles into the deep forest canopy, happy to blend in. While we run around consuming energy and information on a massive scale and creating mounds of waste, the sloth takes a full month to digest a leaf with its internal fermentation gases. While our lives seem to get faster and faster every day, the sloth is happy to go at its own glacial pace. Slowing down, resting, relaxing, and sleeping have become luxuries for many of us. The sloth reminds us that all of these are necessary parts of our lives.

Sloths in the wild sleep for eight or nine hours because they have to be on the lookout for predators. But in captivity in a less stressful environment, they have been known to sleep up to twenty hours a day. They are famously slow, moving through the trees with a fluid, graceful, but to us agonizingly snaillike, pace.

A big part of using animal wisdom is imagining ourselves in the bodies and lives of different animals, and when we do this with the sloth, we can appreciate the brilliance of their slowness. The idea that the sloth is lazy is actually an outdated and unhelpful myth. Sloths use their lack of speediness as a defense mechanism; quick-moving prey easily catch the eye of various predators. The languid, gentle movements of sloths blend in perfectly with the undulating vitality of the rain forest. Sloths also have a cooperative relationship with a certain type of algae that camouflages their color and smell, and their fur plays host to a wide variety of insects, making them seem more plantlike than animal and bringing new meaning to the power of cooperation and creative self-defense.

Like the old myth about the sloth, we may have inadvertently adopted a story about ourselves, an agreement, that taking time for ourselves to rest, nap, or do nothing is a sign of terrible laziness. We may have decided we are only worthwhile when we are busy. But rest, relaxation, and good sleep are not just necessary for our physical health, they're also critical to our ability to fully relate to the world, to each other, and to our inner selves. We may want to slow down but not know how. All the more reason to try to invoke the teachings of the sloth into your life whenever you can.

Questions to Consider

- Are you getting enough rest and relaxation? What are some ways you can take a significant break right now? Can you take a few minutes to nap or spend time just hanging out in nature?

- Has life gotten ahead of you? Do you feel rushed and exhausted? How can you slow down and appreciate the present moment?

- When was the last time you simply sat and did nothing?

Calling the Spirit of the Sloth

One obvious way to connect with the spirit of the sloth is to spend some time actively doing nothing at all. This is harder than it sounds, and very different than taking a nap or meditating, though both of those activities are also in keeping with the spirit of the sloth. Doing nothing goes against everything we may have been taught growing up about the importance of keeping busy and accomplishing important things. In addition, doing nothing can be boring, and our society has developed something of an allergic reaction to boredom. Our phones entertain us on command, and we reach for them long before boredom sets in. But boredom is also the wellspring of new ideas, creativity, and inspiration. We could all benefit from a little extra boredom.

Try to find fifteen or twenty minutes out of your day to start. Turn off your phone, TV, and any other electronic devices, and put away any book you may be reading. Turn off music or podcasts, and just . . . be. Since we've made staving off boredom such a habit, boredom may take this opportunity to come roaring back with a vengeance. You may be immediately overcome with the urge to get up and do something, or you may feel a surge of anxiety or even fear. That's okay. Say a prayer and ask the sloth to help you slow down and access a different relationship to your spiritual and creative life. See if you can incorporate a period of doing nothing into your weekly or even daily routine. It might become something you truly look forward to: a time of peace, rest, and imagination and a refreshing vacation for your spirit, mind, and soul.

A Prayer for Sloth Energy

Friend sloth, moving with studied grace
through the trees, teach me how
to slow down so that I may hear
the whispered words of Mother Earth
at the deep and nourishing pace of real life.

SPARROW

Teachings to Remember When Encountering Sparrows

Highly adaptable, with a wide range of food sources, sparrows can be found just about anywhere. They are so common and nondescript that, together with a number of wrens and finches, some birders jokingly call them "little brown birds," or LBBs. That's in fact one facet of their animal medicine. Unless you're excited about exploring their particular attributes in order to identify them out in the wild, it's fine to be content with their basicness when you commune with them. Still, the sparrow teaches that sameness can be a way to hide in plain sight and allow only those with a real interest to appreciate what's special about each individual. After all, the world's diversity includes the subtle markings of the humble sparrow just as much as the thrilling colors of the peacock. Paying mindful attention to details can be a challenge in our fast-paced world, but it reaps incredible rewards.

See Also: Nightingale

Related animals: chickadee, cowbird, finch, grosbeak, junco, wren

Element: air

- Detail-oriented
- Simple and humble
- Ordinary

Sparrows gather in large numbers and poke around everywhere looking for food, from front yards to plates of food on outdoor patios. You can fill an hour or an afternoon watching them cheerfully hopping, squabbling with each other, puffing their feathers, and flitting from branch to branch, their shiny eyes constantly alert to what's happening around them.

They're not very colorful, and many sparrows don't even have a song to sing. They merely peep. There are teachings even in this. While we feel called and even pushed to make our lives as loud and unique as possible, there is a rich mysticism in the ordinary and the everyday, the drab and the unremarkable, that goes unnoticed in today's society. Like the tiny seeds they primarily eat, sparrows embody the grace of simplicity and the importance of the day-to-day. It takes faith, patience, and vision to tune in to things that aren't flashy, quick, or intense. But changing our focus in this way humbles us, and offers the unending reward of loving the ordinary.

Questions to Consider

- Have things started to look the same in an area of your life? What are you missing? Can you refresh your commitment to noticing the details?

- What simple pleasure do you most enjoy? How can you reclaim quiet peace of mind amid such a busy, chaotic culture like ours?

Calling the Spirit of the Sparrow

From religious traditions to cultural and ecological practices, the simplicity movement is as strong as ever. To connect with the humble ordinariness of the little sparrow, consider how you might simplify your life, pay attention to the small moments, and honor the familiar. Consider something you see every day and never give a second thought: the doorway to your kitchen, a pair of scissors, an old wooden spoon. Think of an event that happens daily or seasonally that passes by unnoticed: the predawn quiet, the subtle shift from summer to fall. Take just a few moments to appreciate these small things, noting them in your journal.

Gratitude for the basics can also give you a fresh outlook. A friend of mine hates doing the dishes, but she found a way to enjoy the experience by paying attention to the feel of the warm water, the pleasant smell of the dish soap, as well as the shape and color of the dishes themselves.

You might also consider clearing out some clutter or downsizing your possessions. This is one basic form of simplicity, but it's only the beginning. Whenever we pause to consider our words before speaking, choose to spend an evening at home with loved ones instead of going out, or just turn off our phones and sit in silence, we are participating in the grounded simplicity of the sparrow.

A Prayer for Sparrow Energy

Little brown bird, small and plain,
reveal the silent simplicity of a kind word
or a handful of seeds. Help me to see
the wonder that dwells in the heart
of even the humblest things.

SPIDER

See Also: Coyote, Crow, Fox, Rabbit

Related animals: lacewing, raven, silkworm

Elements: fire and earth

- Expressive
- Interconnected and interdependent
- Assertive

Teachings to Remember When Encountering Spiders

Like snakes, spiders can inspire an instinctual jump when we see them, or for some even genuine terror. With all those extra legs, fanglike "jaws," and the ability to scurry around or drop down on us from above without warning, it makes sense. Our ancient knowing tells us to be wary of a venomous bite that can be dangerous, unlikely though it may be. When we slow down and look closely, mastering our initial panic response, spiders become fascinating creatures. They are the great web builders, giving us the very notion of a web of all life. An essential part of this web themselves, throughout history spiders have been revered in spiritual traditions and depicted in various forms of art.

Several indigenous cultures in the Americas associate the spider with creation and creativity. For example, the Diné (Navajo) and Hopi people of the American Southwest honor a goddess called Spider Woman or Spider Grandmother, who created the world and is a helper to the people who live in it. Other cultures in the Americas and in Africa consider the spider a trickster, like the coyote and the raven. And many ancient civilizations associated the spider with weaving, creation, fate, and destiny.

The spider has a wealth of teachings to impart to those who are brave enough to approach it with respect. Close your eyes and image a spider's orb web in the morning, when beads of dew cling to each strand and make it shimmer in the light. We stand in awe of the spider's ability to create something that is seemingly so delicate and ephemeral, a pattern improvised on the fly and executed to perfection, a home built from the strong, sticky substance that comes from the spider's own body. Spider silk is lighter than cotton but has a tensile strength as strong as steel. In the spider's web, we see all the ways in which we are connected and interdependent with others in the living world. Pull on one thread, and the whole thing moves. The spider teaches us that if we move with an awareness of how the world is connected, draw on our natural strengths, and repair as we go, we can be the weaver and architect of our own life in a way that seems effortless and light but creates lasting bonds of beauty and strength.

Questions to Consider

- Take some time to think about the vast interconnectedness of your life—the web of family, colleagues, friends, acquaintances, and even the influence of ancestors and how you might affect the future through your creative expression, your actions, and your descendants.

- Do you feel like the artist/architect of your life? What are some ways you can start to build your web with a more solid intent?

Calling the Spirit of the Spider

All weaving and textile art belongs to the spirit of the spider. One way to connect symbolically to the spider's wisdom is by weaving while meditating on the deeper teachings of the spider in your life. This activity can be as simple as find-ing three strands of yarn or string, tying a knot in the end, and braiding them into a small bracelet. Alternatively, there are many, many different methods and techniques of weaving to explore on the internet and at your local library, and several friends have learned to weave using simple tabletop or portable looms. The rhythmic nature of weaving and braiding can often deepen the meditative state of mind. You may consider chanting while you work, perhaps by using the rhythmic prayer given below, which will only deepen the experience.

Another way to call spider medicine into your life is to draw and label a web in your journal. You can use this drawing to map the interconnectedness of the people in your life, the structure of a project at home or work, or as a way to get a different look at your to-do list. Alternatively, you might want to start with a problem or question at the center of your web, label it, and then draw the radial lines traveling out from the center. Label each of these with issues or considerations that affect this problem. Finally, fill in some of the cross-webbing, naming the people, places, things, and time scales at play. Really try to get everything out of your head and onto paper in this web. Set your drawing aside for a few days, then come back to it to see if it reveals new information or helps you make any useful connections.

A Prayer for Spider Energy

Spider friend, spider teacher,
spinning wonder from your heart,
help me weave the threads of fate,
to craft my life as sacred art.

SQUIRREL

Teachings to Remember When Encountering Squirrels

Squirrels are one of those animals that we might take for granted since we see them so often. Whether in rural or urban environments, it seems like squirrels are just everywhere, and they can frustrate us by gnawing their way into our homes or eating seeds out of our garden beds. But like other highly adaptable animals, squirrels are hardy, resourceful, and incredibly persistent, and they're worthy of our attention. Additionally, for those living in dense urban areas, pigeons, sparrows, rats, and squirrels provide some of our only opportunities to connect with wildlife on a regular basis. In fact, during the nineteenth century, squirrels were nearly eradicated from New York City, but were later reintroduced to Central Park to bring joy and entertainment to city residents.

Squirrels are very inquisitive and curious, especially when it comes to finding new ways to scavenge for food, but one of their most valuable lessons is in how persistent they are. You can probably find any one of thousands of stories, possibly from your own neighbors, about the determination of squirrels when it comes to climbing seemingly impossible structures, finding their way into

See Also: Opossum

Related animals: chipmunk, flying squirrel, fox squirrel, groundhog, marmot, mouse, prairie dog, red squirrel, vole

Element: earth

- Curious and determined
- Ready
- Grounded

closed up spaces, opening bird feeders that are supposed to be "squirrel-proof," and waiting in trees and along the tops of fences for pet dogs to leave the area so they can survey the yard for food. They will show up, again and again, until their mission is accomplished.

The determination of showing up is a critical part of a creative life, a business life, a social life, and even a spiritual life. Learning new things or trying to reach a far-off goal can be overwhelming and painful. We may want to give up. If we shift to a more attainable goal of simply sitting down and showing up with readiness, we can surprise ourselves by how much comes to us as if by magic. After all, squirrels diligently lay away mountains of acorns and nuts every fall. They don't know what will happen in the future—the squirrel is focused on the action, not the outcome. They have no way of knowing that the long-term outcome of a forgotten acorn stash may well be a new acorn tree to feed their ancestors.

Making a daily goal and sticking to it, even if you don't know the outcome or can't control it, is a powerful practice of intention. Writing every day in a journal without exception, even if everything you write is nonsense, eventually gives way to inspiration. When you feel like you just might be at the very end of your ability to be creative, inspired, or see something through to the end, call on the spirit of the determined squirrel to help you focus on the present and show up, ready to go.

Questions to Consider

- Are you at the end of your patience with a project or situation? How might you focus on what you *can* do in the present?

- Is there a subject you've been curious about for some time but haven't really delved into? How can you channel the inquisitiveness and perseverance of the squirrel to help you learn more about this topic?

Calling the Spirit of the Squirrel

Showing up can also be a simple means of grounding yourself in nature. Even in the middle of a city, when we show up regularly and look at the same patch of earth—in a park, a backyard, or even a traffic median—we notice all sorts of things: the shifting of the seasons and the quality of light, the differences in flora and fauna, the amount of change and movement. The idea is to make a regular habit of visiting one area and taking pictures, sketching, or making notes about what you observe that day or that week. Sometimes it will seem like nothing's going on at all. That's okay. The point is to dedicate yourself to this place and show up for a significant period of time. After a while, you will become so in tune with your spot that it will be *you* that changes, as your awareness and observational skills deepen. You may start to notice differences in moisture levels in the soil and how that affects the color of the foliage around you. You may see variations in the markings on what you thought were all the same brown bird. By showing up consistently to this spot, you are not only offering the place the sacred gift of your attention, you are receiving a gift from the living world as it opens up to your keen perception and perseverance. When it feels right and appropriate, gather something small from this place for your altar at home: an acorn or leaf, a bit of earth, or a dried flower.

A Prayer for Squirrel Energy

Friend squirrel, determined and curious,
help me to keep showing up, to give this project,
this life, the careful and persistent attention it
deserves. Teach me how to pursue a relationship
with the living world with a tenacious joy.

SWAN

See Also: Crane, Goose

Related animals: duck, heron

Elements: air and water

- Monogamous
- Evolving
- Graceful

Teachings to Remember When Encountering Swans

Swans possess an inherent beauty and wild grace that have captivated humankind for centuries and put them at the center of mythological and spiritual stories from ancient Greece, Ireland, Scandinavia, and the Hindu Vedic scriptures. Their natural, fluid movement aligns with divinity and the ability to navigate between worlds. Swans normally bond for life, and thus have become a symbol for romance. There is an even deeper wisdom if we relate these two qualities of divinity and pairing. The swan's grace can represent a being who has achieved a certain level of wholeness of self—in other words, a person who is bonded for life to their own truest nature. We all crave authentic connection and deep relationships, and bonding with different people over the course of a lifetime is one of the great gifts of being human. But the swan also embodies the notion of bonding with our true authentic self. We can become our own soul mates!

Most people know the story of "The Ugly Duckling" by Hans Christian Andersen, in which an ungainly little duckling grows up to discover that he is in fact a beautiful swan. As I see it, this fable is in many ways about how we adopt the agreements given to us by society as we grow up. As a young creature, the duckling hears that he is too large and strange, so he can't fit in as a "real" duck. He adopts these notions into his internal belief system. As young people, we may hear we are too loud, too awkward, too tall, or that our dreams are too big for us to accomplish. On a subconscious level, we may agree to these ideas and come to believe that they are true, when the real truth is that our authentic selves are absolutely good enough just as they are. By working to ferret out and confront our agreements, we can come to see that we are all in fact swans ourselves.

Questions to Consider

- How can you cultivate more grace in your life? What physical activities, such as yoga, dance, or qigong, would you maybe want to try to this end?

- Do you have any soul mates in your life? These don't have to be romantic partners—they could include friends and chosen family with whom you connect deeply.

- Do you consider yourself a soul mate to your own inner authentic self?

Calling the Spirit of the Swan

We all may wish for more grace in our lives. Grace can mean many things: physical coordination, a sense of innate kindness, or an ever-present divinity. To connect with the spirit of the swan, especially in light of its teachings on the inner authentic self, consider these various definitions of grace and how you might already embody them on a regular basis, as well as how you may enhance these attributes even more. Natural grace often arises from a deep-seated trust and connection with one's inner self. Grace seems instinctive in so many wild animals because they have no use for the self-criticism we immerse ourselves in on a regular basis. Their wildness connects them fundamentally to their physical being, to the earth. As you work on divining how you may embody grace in your life, call on the spirit of the beautiful, grace-filled swan to assist you.

A Prayer for Swan Energy

Friend swan, imbued with wild grace,
help me to become soul mates with my
innermost authentic self. Teach me how
to let my true being shine like a great light
over water—to radiate outward and to offer
kindness, strength, and beauty wherever I go.

TURTLE

Related animals: armadillo, mollusk, sea turtle, snail

Elements: water and earth

- Wise
- Prepared
- Patient and trusting

Teachings to Remember When Encountering Turtles

The great turtle, who carries the world on its enormous shell, graces the founding mythologies of many North American indigenous cultures, as well as those of India and China. Turtle and tortoise embody slow patience, wisdom, time itself, and well-protected softness. These animals remind us to take things slow, relish peace, fortify our strength, and build our inner and outer realities with diligence.

Though it looks from the outside like the turtle is carrying its shell, in fact its spine is fused to the shell itself. They do not carry their protective home; they *are* their protective home. The medicine here is that while we may believe that our home is separate from us, the building where we hang our hat or keep our stuff, the truth is that our real home lives within—as much a part of us as our own bones. This is the home of the self, a place of protection inside of which we can be soft and supple, focused and strong.

Tortoises live longer than any animal on earth. The oldest one alive today, named Jonathan, lives on the island of Saint Helena and hatched in 1832. Aging brings powerful wisdom and knowledge born of experience, and in many ways our current cultural stories have forgotten the power of aging as more and more people become obsessed with preventing aging in any way possible. The turtle reminds us that aging bodies and minds can and do grow stronger in ways we might never expect in our youth. Instead of bypassing this critical stage of life, we can discover it with fresh eyes and attend to the teaching and sharing that are natural during this time. The turtle can lead the way as spiritual master, helping us trust the steady movement of time and the aging process.

Questions to Consider

- What stage of life are you in? Are you embracing it fully, or are you resisting it?

- What does home mean to you? Do you feel at ease in your own body? What about in yourself? What can you do to welcome yourself home and to carry your home in your heart?

- Is there an elder in your life that you look to for wisdom? Is there a question in your heart you can bring to them at this time?

Calling the Spirit of the Turtle

The turtle helps us slow down and come into the unfolding present moment, even as we remain aware of the passage of time. Especially when you are feeling distracted or agitated, it can be very powerful to add a turtle totem to your medicine bag or personal altar or even slip a small carved turtle figure into your pocket. Then, whenever you feel rushed or harried, or think that you have to react right away to a situation or problem in front of you, gently touch or hold the turtle talisman. Take a deep breath and remember to take things more slowly. There is always time.

Another wise and powerful teaching of the turtle has to do with your own aging process. You may be young still and have a lot of aging left to do, or you may be making your way into later stages of your lifetime. What do you fear about aging? Is it death? The loss of certain capacities or potential? How is this fear stopping you from enjoying or being curious about this natural process and embracing it as part of a life well-lived? Can you envision the most wonderful version of your wise old self? Who is with you? What colors do you wear? What books do you read? What skill has become second nature to you? What brings you comfort and what excites your imagination? Perhaps most importantly, how do you relay your wisdom in service to others?

Finally, I encourage you to connect with elders who are friends or family members. Spend regular, meaningful time with them. Ask them questions and lean in for the answers. In every wrinkle and line of their face and hands there is wisdom, just as there is in the great ancient tortoise, who carries the whole world on its sturdy, patient back.

A Prayer for Turtle Energy

Ancient one, wise tortoise,
witness through the ages; help me
to let go of my clinging to youth and
embrace the power and knowledge
that comes with age. Teach me how
to listen to the wisdom that lives
always in the home of my heart.

VULTURE

Teachings to Remember When Encountering Vultures

Vultures have long been both revered and loathed. Ancient Egypt revered a vulture goddess named Nekhbet, who is often depicted as a vulture holding the Egyptian symbol of protection. Naturally, as carrion eaters, vultures have been associated with death, battlefields, and war, but they serve a critical ecological function by cleaning up and recycling organic matter that would otherwise spread bacteria and disease.

See also: Beetle, Coyote, Opossum, Komodo Dragon

Related animals: condor, maggot

Elements: air and earth

- Transformative
- Protective and restorative
- Balanced

With their naked necks and heads and their hunched over appearance, we don't often think of vultures as majestic or beautiful. They also may stink; in addition to hanging around decomposing material, turkey vultures defecate on their feet to cool them off. Some vultures also projectile vomit in response to threats. So it might be hard to see why we would look to them for any kind of wisdom. Yet they do still glide beautifully on thermal air currents through the clear blue sky, and have many teachings to offer about the realities of mortal life, as well as the importance of balance, cleansing, and recycling. Vultures teach us how to embrace our physical selves as real, organic parts of nature. The animals that are ignored or disliked can hold some of the most powerful lessons, since they show us what we fear and do not want to face. Very often, they reveal unexpected and potent ways toward healing.

All animals die, just as you and I and everyone else will eventually die, and our physical bodies will return to the earth. If our bodies are exposed to the air, vultures and other animals will eat us. If they are burned, they release energy and molecules that get recycled in turn. If we're buried in the earth, we'll be eaten by something else. Death does not have to be gruesome; it's a simple fact of life. Facing the fact of death can help foster deep respect for the limited time we have to live. No matter what happens to our conscious mind, spirit, or soul when we die, vulture medicine reminds us that our body belongs to Mother Earth and will always be a part of the great cycle of life. We eat, we die, we feed others. This beautiful dance sustains life on our finite planet.

Vultures are creatures of air, which is associated with clarity and the mind. Because of their relationship to death, decay, and regeneration, they are also creatures of earth and remind us of our physical body. The vulture reminds us not to push away thoughts of death and mortality but to honor this fact of life and come to an inner peace and clarity of vision that is transformative and freeing.

Questions to Consider

- What do you consider ugly, dirty, or imperfect in yourself? What would it take to see these same qualities as majestic?

- How can you apply a "spring cleaning" to those areas of your life that need a fresh perspective? Would a literal cleaning of your home be of benefit? Or would cleansing on an inner, spiritual level help, perhaps through ritual or prayer?

- Is a project or relationship out of balance? How can you use the energies of recycling and renewal to bring it back into balance?

Calling the Spirit of the Vulture

There are different species of vultures everywhere. The next time you're in an open space, try to spot them spiraling high in the air. They may also be found hanging around the side of the road. Consider taking up the practice of offering a small prayer for any animals you see that have been killed by cars. Call to the spirit of the vulture and other carrion eaters to come and help it transform into nourishment for others and return to the arms of its Mother Earth. It's natural to mourn in the face of death, while also acknowledging that death is a sacred and necessary part of life.

You may also want to meditate on your own mortality. This may sound morbid, but it can actually be very peaceful and healthy. The Buddhist meditation on death is called *maranasati*, and some Buddhists are expected to think about death five times a day. Talking about death and dying with family members can also be a powerful, life-affirming experience. It might be hard to get started, but it can be very reassuring to clear the air and have a frank and honest conversation with your loved ones—from the practical side of living wills and funeral arrangements to more spiritual conversations about what you believe happens to the mind and soul after death. There are some great resources available online to assist you in having these conversations in a respectful and positive way. Before you do, call in the spirit of the vulture to guide you in seeking this important balance.

A Prayer for Vulture Energy

Sacred vulture, keeper of the balance,
soaring as high as your cousin the hawk
yet remaining grounded in the truth of death,
teach me how to accept my own mortality
with grace and a clear mind.

WHALE

The great and powerful whale is a wise ancestral teacher, majestic deep diver, and protector of family. Playful and gentle, fierce and formidable, whales all over the world leave us humbled and in awe. There is something almost unfathomable about the whale's physical and spiritual presence. For example, it's hard to picture the immensity of the blue whale, the largest living creature on earth, and in fact larger than any animal that has *ever* lived on earth. Its heart alone is as big as a car, with a heartbeat that can be heard two miles away.

See also: Elephant, Hippopotamus

Related animals: beluga whale, blue whale, humpback whale, narwhal, orca

Element: water

• Contemplative and peaceful
• Emotional
• Communicative

Watching videos or looking at images of this animal, we feel our heart and mind become calm and peaceful in their gliding, gentle presence. Listening to the eerie, amazing songs of the humpback whale brings a sense of ease and connection.

Whales are mammals who spend their entire lives in the sea, often in matrilineal pods. This is a beautiful metaphor for choosing to dive deep into the emotional richness of our lives within the reciprocal loving care of our families—chosen and not. Orcas, for one, never leave their mothers, and mating involves a complex ritual of matchmaking presided over by the grandmothers of two separate pods.

Whales, like tortoises, are both slow and long-lived. Many of them navigate extensive migratory patterns each year. While the inner lives of whales may be unknown to us, these attributes create the potential for a deep understanding over great distances of time and space. There is a group of gray whales who give birth to their calves in Baja, Mexico. Commercial whaling was common in this area until the middle of last century, and the whales in the area were understandably aggressive toward boats and people and protective of their young. But within thirty years of closing down the whale stations, some of the same individual whales, who are old enough to remember the whaling industry, have graciously come to connect with humans again. In fact, this pod is known as the Friendlies because of their willingness to interact in mutual respect and gentleness with humans who visit them.

Whale medicine teaches us how to slow down, appreciate the world around us, and float in the present moment, resting in the vast arms of the universe. In her book *A Stroke of Insight*, neuroscientist Jill Bolte Taylor describes her experience of having a stroke. After experiencing intense pain, she says she "felt like a genie liberated from its bottle." Her spirit "seemed to flow like a great whale gliding through a sea of silent euphoria." She'd found nirvana. Whale wisdom hints at the vast and ineffable mystery of consciousness itself, of reality beyond what we know with our storytelling mind.

Questions to Consider

- Are you willing to take a life-giving breath and dive deep into emotional waters?

- Is there something in your heart that you haven't shared with someone else—something that would unburden you to release? How can you tap into the vast, contemplative peace of the whale to guide you toward your next step?

- What is your relationship to your own mother? Whether painful or fulfilled, working with whale medicine can bring a sense of belonging, nurturing, and deep emotional connection. Can you think of a way to honor and heal the mother/child relationships in your life?

Calling the Spirit of the Whale

As with many animals, meditation can draw the spirit of this ancient, wise teacher into your life. You may also want to add an image of a whale or whale tail to your personal altar or some other symbol to your medicine bag. To call the spirit of the whale during meditation, spend some time contemplating and imagining what it may feel like to drift through the deep blue open water or even through the vast unknowable reaches of space, unbothered and unhurried. Let all your past worries and future anxieties drift out and away from you, falling slowly down to the ocean floor where they will be recycled, forgotten, and forgiven. You can even meditate in this way in the bath or while floating in a pool or other body of water, allowing the feeling of weightlessness to support your exploration.

A Prayer for Whale Energy

Mother whale, drifting through
the vast blue enormity of the sea,
help me to navigate the depths of my being
with your same grace. Teach me
to make my life into a song that echoes
the wisdom of timeless peace into every moment.

WOLF

See also: Dog, Coyote, Fox

Related animals: dingo, hyena, jackal, wild dog

Element: earth

- Team-oriented
- Passionate
- Swift, strong, and brave

Teachings to Remember When Encountering Wolves

Every culture that has encountered the wolf tells stories that inspire respect, fear, and admiration for these fierce predators and protectors of family and territory. For many, including many Native American cultures, the wolf symbolizes strength, hunting ability, social bonding, bravery, and swiftness. Hunting in packs, loyal to their family group, and working together as a team, their skills are legendary. Warriors and soldiers call on the wolf to inspire feats of bravery and solidarity.

Close your eyes and hear the otherworldly howl of the wolf, see it silhouetted against a full moon on a winter night. Wolves don't actually howl at the moon; instead, they use their voices to connect with their pack over long distances. But the moon is still a potent and resonant aspect of their symbolic power. It makes sense to consider the full moon's beauty and ceremonial importance as a part of the teachings of the wolf.

Wolves are social creatures who mate for life. Sometimes we hear about a "lone wolf," a character both idolized and feared in our cultural stories. Because wolves travel and bond together in packs, a solitary wolf may be both vulnerable and highly dangerous to others. But being a lone wolf is more a temporary condition than a character trait, as they are likely to join another pack or start one of their own. Lone wolf medicine can help us when we are in transition, reminding us to honor the sacredness of time spent away from the pack. Exploring and expanding territory—whether outward or inward—is an important part of life, but so is the return to community and the commitment to maintaining family and social bonds. Working in this way, we come into the full expression of wolf power.

Wolves are in the earth quadrant of the medicine wheel, the element of solidity, groundedness, connection, and physical strength. Call on the wolf to reconnect you to the earth.

Questions to Consider

- What is your heart's desire? What are some ways you might begin to focus your awareness, the gifts of the hunter, on achieving this ultimate dream?

- Who in your life makes up your pack? How might you reach out to them to help you achieve your goals? And what are some ways you might lend them support? Are there community goals you can all work toward together?

- When was the last time you went outdoors during a full moon? How would working toward your dreams in alignment with the energy of the waxing and waning moon help you achieve your heart's desire?

Calling the Spirit of the Wolf

Connect with the spirit of the wolf by spending time in the presence of the moon, with friends and family, or with a small group of colleagues or friends.

Live out wolf symbolism in a concrete way by shouting with joy, laughing out loud, or singing with your friends. To connect with the gift of the lone wolf, consider spending some time away from others on purpose, for as little as an afternoon or as long as a few days. This period of isolation has a rich history in many different spiritual traditions and can inspire clarity, concentration, and insight. Then give thanks for the joy in reconnecting with your pack when your time as a lone wolf is over.

A Prayer for Wolf Energy

Hunter wolves on the moonlit mountain,
working swiftly together as a whole,
lend us your strength, your focus.
Teach us to be brave, to care for one another,
to work together toward a common goal.

INDEX OF ANIMALS

lark, 145
lemur, 139
leopard, 124, 133
Lion, 133
lizard, 30
lovebird, 86
lynx, 53, 124, 133

macaque, 139
maggot, 214
magpie, 74
Malaysian exploding ant, 193
manatee, 83, 98, 115
marmot, 205
minnow, 177
mockingbird, 145
mole rat, 136
Mole, 136
mollusk, 211
mongoose, 148
monitor lizard, 130
moose, 77
Monkey, 139
Moth, 142
mountain goat, 107, 190
mountain lion, 124, 133
mourning dove, 86
mouse, 168, 171, 205
mule, 119
muskrat, 151

narwhal, 217
newt, 104
Nightingale, 145

ocelot, 53

octopus, 56
Opossum, 148
orca, 217
oriole, 145
osprey, 112
Otter 151
Owl, 154
oxen, 65

pacific tree frog, 56
panda, 38
panther, 53
parrot, 74
Peacock, 158
pelican, 180
Penguin, 161
pheasant, 59, 109, 158
Pig, 164
pigeon, 86, 171
pika, 168
pistol shrimp, 193
porcupine, 148, 193
prairie dog, 205
python, 174

quail, 59
Rabbit, 168
Raccoon, 171
rainbow trout, 177
rat, 36, 168, 171
Rattlesnake, 174
raven, 74, 202
red squirrel, 205
reindeer, 77, 119
rhinoceros, 98, 115
rooster, 59

ABOUT THE AUTHOR

Don José Ruiz was born in Mexico City and raised in Tijuana. From a very young age, he was guided by many teachers, including his mother, Maria, his father, don Miguel, and his grandmother Sarita.

As a *Nagual* (the Nahuatl word for shaman), José brings new insights to the ancient wisdom of his family, translating it into practical, everyday life concepts that promote transformation through truth, love, and common sense. José has dedicated his life to sharing this Toltec wisdom, and he travels the world helping others find their own personal truth.

Don José Ruiz is the author of *The Medicine Bag* and *The Wisdom of the Shamans,* and coauthor of *The Fifth Agreement*, which he wrote in collaboration with his father, don Miguel Ruiz, author of *The Four Agreements*.

Also from Hierophant Publishing

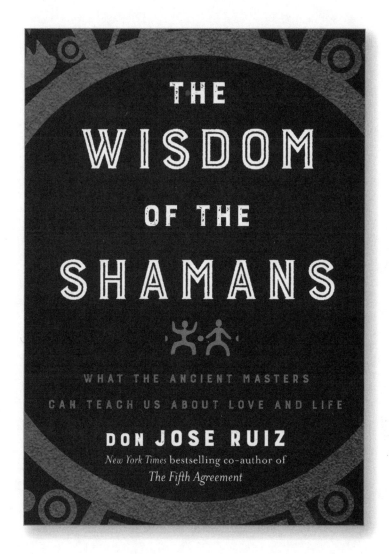

Available wherever books are sold.